MARK TWAIN'S
Huckleberry Finn

BY
Joseph Claro

SERIES EDITOR
Michael Spring
Editor, *Literary Cavalcade*
Scholastic Inc.

BARRON'S EDUCATIONAL SERIES, INC.
New York / London / Toronto / Sydney

ACKNOWLEDGMENTS

We would like to acknowledge the many painstaking hours of work Holly Hughes and Thomas F. Hirsch have devoted to making the *Book Notes* series a success.

All inquiries should be addressed to:
Barron's Educational Series, Inc.
250 Wireless Boulevard
Hauppauge, New York 11788

Library of Congress Catalog Card No. 84-18549

International Standard Book No. 0-8120-3420-1

Library of Congress Cataloging in Publication Data
Claro, Joseph.
  Mark Twain's Huckleberry Finn.

  (Barron's book notes)
  Bibliography: p. 99
  Summary: A guide to reading "Huckleberry Finn" with a
critical and appreciative mind encouraging analysis of
plot, style, form, and structure. Also includes
background on the author's life and times, sample tests,
term paper suggestions, and a reading list.
  1. Twain, Mark, 1835–1910. Adventures of Huckleberry
Finn. [1. Twain, Mark, 1835–1910. Adventures of
Huckleberry Finn. 2. American literature—History
and criticism] I. Title. II. Title: Huckleberry Finn.
III. Series.
PS1305.C55   1984   813'.4   84-18549
ISBN 0-8120-3420-1 (pbk.)

PRINTED IN THE UNITED STATES OF AMERICA

123   550   987654

CONTENTS

ADVISORY BOARD

HOW TO USE THIS BOOK

You have to know how to approach literature in order to get the most out of it. This *Barron's Book Notes* volume follows a plan based on methods used by some of the best students to read a work of literature.

Begin with the guide's section on the author's life and times. As you read, try to form a clear picture of the author's personality, circumstances, and motives for writing the work. This background usually will make it easier for you to hear the author's tone of voice, and follow where the author is heading.

Then go over the rest of the introductory material—such sections as those on the plot, characters, setting, themes, and style of the work. Underline, or write down in your notebook, particular things to watch for, such as contrasts between characters and repeated literary devices. At this point, you may want to develop a system of symbols to use in marking your text as you read. (Of course, you should only mark up a book you own, not one that belongs to another person or a school.) Perhaps you will want to use a different letter for each character's name, a different number for each major theme of the book, a different color for each important symbol or literary device. Be prepared to mark up the pages of your book as you read. Put your marks in the margins so you can find them again easily.

Now comes the moment you've been waiting for—the time to start reading the work of literature. You may want to put aside your *Barron's Book Notes* volume until you've read the work all the way through. Or you may want to alternate, reading the *Book Notes* analysis of each section as soon as you have finished reading the corresponding part of the original. Before you move on, reread crucial passages you don't fully understand. (Don't take this guide's analysis for granted—make up your own mind as to what the work means.)

Once you've finished the whole work of literature, you may want to review it right away, so you can firm up your ideas about what it means. You may want to leaf through the book concentrating on passages you marked in reference to one character or one theme. This is also a good time to reread the *Book Notes* introductory material, which pulls together insights on specific topics.

When it comes time to prepare for a test or to write a paper, you'll already have formed ideas about the work. You'll be able to go back through it, refreshing your memory as to the author's exact words and perspective, so that you can support your opinions with evidence drawn straight from the work. Patterns will emerge, and ideas will fall into place; your essay question or term paper will almost write itself. Give yourself a dry run with one of the sample tests in the guide. These tests present both multiple-choice and essay questions. An accompanying section gives answers to the multiple-choice questions as well as suggestions for writing the essays. If you have to select a term paper topic, you may choose one from the list of suggestions in this book. This guide also provides you with a reading list, to help you when you start research for a term paper, and a selection of provocative comments by critics, to spark your thinking before you write.

THE AUTHOR AND HIS TIMES

In the final paragraph of *The Adventures of Huckleberry Finn*, Huck says, ". . . so there ain't nothing more to write about, and I am rotten glad of it, because if I'd 'a' knowed what a trouble it was to make a book I wouldn't 'a' tackled it, and ain't a-going to no more."

As you'll see when you've read the novel, the sentiment is very much in character for Huck; but you can also read it as an expression of Mark Twain's relief at finishing the most difficult writing task he ever tackled.

The book had taken him more than seven years to complete. At one point he was so frustrated with it that he considered burning what he'd written. Instead, he put it aside and worked on three other books that were published before *Huck Finn*.

Twain finished the book in the summer of 1883, just before his 48th birthday. At the time, he was not only rich, but an internationally known writer and lecturer, doing the best work of his career, and married to a woman he adored. It seems appropriate that he should have written his masterpiece during this period, the best time of his life.

Twain's real name was Samuel Clemens, and he was born in 1835 in Florida, Missouri. When he was four years old, his family moved to Hannibal, a town made famous by his books. (In *The Adventures of Tom Sawyer*, he called the town St. Petersburg. "St. Peter's town" was his way of calling Hannibal heaven.)

He went to work as a printer's assistant when he was 11 years old, just after his father died. After he turned 18, he left Hannibal to work as a printer in St. Louis, then in New York. The printing trade got him interested in writing, and he began submitting pieces to newspapers and magazines while he was still in his teens.

He moved from one town to another, practicing his two trades, reporting and printing. He taught himself to write by writing, and eventually he sold more and more of the things he wrote.

If one thing characterized Twain as a young man, it was the urge to move on, an unwillingness to stay put. (This is one of many traits he has in common with Huck Finn.) In 1857 he decided that South America was the place to get rich. So he got on a riverboat headed for New Orleans, where he would arrange the rest of his trip.

He never made it past New Orleans, however. The trip reminded him of how much he loved not only the Mississippi River, but the riverboats that made up its most impressive traffic. He persuaded the pilot to take him on as an apprentice, and in 1859 he became a full-fledged riverboat pilot himself.

He loved that work, and he might have spent the rest of his life at it if the Civil War hadn't closed the river to trade. He enlisted in the Confederate Army, but he found it hard to take military service seriously. He then went west with his brother and tried mining for gold and silver.

It was during these years in the West that he established himself as a writer. He wrote humorous stories about his experiences, which led to a job as a newspaper reporter in 1862. The following year he began signing his pieces "Mark Twain." The words *mark twain* were a river pilot's phrase that meant two fathoms deep.

In 1866 the travel bug bit him again, and he got his newspaper to send him to Hawaii. This trip was the beginning of his career as a travel correspondent. The following year he traveled through Europe and sent newspaper dispatches back home. These dispatches later became *The Innocents Abroad,* one of the most successful books Twain ever wrote.

His travels resulted not only in a series of books, but in a string of lecture tours that earned him large sums of money and added to his fame. The money and the fame increased even more after he published *The Adventures of Tom Sawyer* in 1876.

That book was such a success that he decided immediately to write a sequel. The sequel, however, evolved into something much more complex than the original book. That's why it took Twain seven years to write it, and why he was so relieved when it was finally finished.

After *Huck Finn,* Twain wrote nearly a dozen books and several shorter pieces. Although none of them would match *Huck Finn* in literary value, his reputation was secure. Unfortunately, other aspects of his life were less benign.

He invested his money in schemes and inventions, almost every one of which was a failure. By 1893 he had lost all his money, and he owed thousands more. He then went on a world lecture tour that allowed him to pay all his debts by 1896.

One of his daughters died while he was on the tour. He then depended more than ever on his wife, and she died in 1904. In 1909 his youngest daughter died, leaving Twain a sick and unhappy man.

Twain used to enjoy pointing out that Halley's

Comet was blazing across the sky when he was born. When he was in a macabre mood, he would sometimes predict that Halley's Comet would announce his departure. The comet made its next appearance in the third week of April, 1910. Mark Twain died on April 21.

"All modern American literature comes from one book by Mark Twain called *Huckleberry Finn*." That might sound like something a teacher would say to catch your interest; but in fact it was said by one of the giants of 20th-century American literature—Ernest Hemingway.

He didn't mean that no Americans before Mark Twain had written anything worthy of being called literature. What he meant was that Twain was responsible for defining what would make American literature different from everybody else's literature. Twain was the first major writer to use real American speech (and not only in dialogue), to deal with themes and topics that were important to Americans, and to assume that the concerns of Americans were as worthy of serious treatment as any ideas that ever sailed across the Atlantic from Britain.

One of the reasons we classify some writers as great is that they alter the consciousness of the people they write for; another is that they redefine the terrain for all writers who come after them. On both counts, Mark Twain is a shoo-in.

He made Americans aware of their surroundings and their heritage. And in defiance of the stilted, formal literary conventions of his day, he made it respectable to feature a hero who could barely read and write, whose language was peppered with decidedly unliterary expressions and figures of speech, and who would probably be out of place in the living rooms of most of the readers of the novel.

Twain's reputation doesn't rest exclusively on *The Adventures of Huckleberry Finn*. *Life on the Mississippi*, *Pudd'nhead Wilson*, and his *Autobiography*, not to mention dozens of shorter pieces, include some of the best writing ever done by an American in any period. But *Huck Finn*, even with its flaws, is his masterpiece— more penetrating, more moving, and better sustained than anything else he wrote.

If he's one of our best writers, and this is his best book, then it has a special place in American history. You don't have to agree with Hemingway's statement to see that someone who hasn't read *Huck Finn* has only a partial understanding of what it means to be an American in the 20th century. The book affected everything that came after it.

But *Huck Finn* is not only important, it's also great fun to read. Twain himself once said, "Everybody wants to have read the classics, but nobody wants to read them." *Huck Finn* is one classic to which his statement doesn't apply.

THE NOVEL

The Plot

Huck introduces himself as someone who appeared in an earlier book by Mark Twain, reminding us of what happened at the end of that story. Though he won't mention it until Chapter 3, his irresponsible father has left him on his own. Huck has been living with Widow Douglas, a kind woman who wants to teach him all the things his father has neglected, the things all normal kids learn.

He tells us about Miss Watson, the widow's sister, who is bent on teaching him manners and religion, and about Tom Sawyer, a boy Huck looks up to because of his wide reading and vivid imagination. He's also friendly with Jim, Miss Watson's black slave.

Huck's father returns and takes him away from the widow. When his father begins beating him too often, Huck runs away and makes it look as though he's been murdered. He hides out on a nearby island, intending to take off after his neighbors stop searching for his body.

Jim is also hiding on the island, since he has run away from Miss Watson, who was about to sell him and separate him from his wife and children. They decide to escape together, and when they find a large raft, their journey along the Mississippi River begins.

After a couple of adventures on the river, their raft is hit by a steamboat, and Huck and Jim are separated. Huck goes ashore and finds himself at the home of the

Grangerfords, who allow him to come and live with them. At first he admires these people for what he thinks is their class and good taste. But when he learns about the deaths caused by a feud with another family, he becomes disgusted with them.

By this time Jim has repaired the raft, and Huck rejoins him. They're soon joined by two men who are escaping the law and who claim to be a duke and the son of the king of France. Huck knows they're actually small-time con men, but he pretends to believe them.

After watching these frauds bilk people of their money in two towns, Huck is forced to help them try to swindle an inheritance out of three girls who were recently orphaned. He goes along at first because he doesn't want them to turn Jim in, but eventually he decides that the thieves have gone too far. He invents a complicated plan to escape and to have them arrested.

The plan almost works, but at the last minute the two crooks show up and continue to travel with Huck and Jim. When all their money-making schemes begin to fail, they sell Jim to a farmer in one of the towns they're visiting. Huck learns about this and decides to free his friend.

The farmer turns out to be Tom Sawyer's uncle, and through a misunderstanding he and his wife think Huck is Tom. When Tom himself arrives, Huck brings him up to date on what's happening. Tom pretends to be his own brother Sid, and the two boys set about to rescue Jim.

True to his imaginative style, Tom devises a plan that is infinitely more complicated than it has to be. Eventually they actually pull it off and reach the raft without being caught. Tom, however, has been shot in the leg, and Jim refuses to leave until the wound has been treated.

The result is that Jim is recaptured and Tom and Huck have to explain what they've done. Tom, it turns out, knew all along that Miss Watson had set Jim free in her will, so everyone can now return home together. Huck, however, thinks he's had enough of civilization, and hints that he might take off for the Indian Territory instead of going back home.

The Characters

Huck tells us about several people who live in his town, and he meets many more on his river voyage. You'll find comments on these characters as Huck introduces them. For an idea in advance of who the main characters are, the following sketches will be helpful.

Huckleberry Finn

Huck is the son of the town drunkard, a man who goes away for long stretches and beats his son when he's home. Huck cares for himself most of the time, though he's living with a charitable woman when the novel begins. He prefers living in the woods to being in a home, and he doesn't think much of school, religious training, or being "sivilized" in general.

When he's in trouble, Huck can be a first-class liar, but generally he's honest, sensitive about other people's feelings, and kind. He sometimes has feelings of guilt over troubles he hasn't caused, and he has a very active and intrusive conscience.

Huck has an ambivalent attitude toward himself. On the one hand, he keeps telling us that he knows he's "low-down" and "ornery," that he's lacking in all the things that make other people respectable. On the other hand, he almost always goes his own way, makes up his own mind, and lives by his own standards.

His negative feelings about himself stem from his belief that certain qualities make people good—such things as education, religious training, and a willingness to follow rules. He's been taught to equate these things with virtue, and the part of his mind that believes in the equation tells him he doesn't measure up.

What he doesn't realize, even at the end of the book, is that goodness is an inner quality, and that it may have no connection to the kind of upbringing someone has had, or even to outward behavior. If Huck understood this point, he'd be more interested in changing society than in running away from it. But because he accepts what he's been taught, he sees himself as an outsider and he would rather run away.

Jim

Jim is a slave owned by Miss Watson, the sister of the woman who's caring for Huck. He has a wife and small children, and the threat of being separated from them frightens him enough to make him run away from his owner before she can sell him. Jim is illiterate, superstitious, and afraid of unnamed forces, characteristics that are the subject of some of the comedy in the book. But he's also tender, sensitive, loyal, and capable of very deep feeling. In some scenes he seems more childish than Huck; in others he's an adult for Huck to rely on.

To some readers, Jim is the most interesting character in the book. He's important to the plot because he gives Huck a reason to travel on the river, and his outlaw status makes it necessary for Huck to keep silent at times when he wants to stop some kind of injustice. But Jim is more than a plot device. He's also the person who brings Huck to a series of important moral decisions.

Because Jim is much more than a stereotypical slave, Huck develops a deep feeling of loyalty toward him. And in spite of Jim's simplicity, naïveté, and childish superstitions, Twain is able to use him as a vehicle for a powerful indictment of the institution of slavery.

Tom Sawyer

Tom is a friend of Huck, a boy Huck admires for his wide reading, unbridled imagination, and flair. An expert at self-promotion, Tom appoints himself leader of a gang dedicated to robbing and killing.

Unlike Huck, Tom is a dreamer, a weaver of fantastic tales and grand schemes. Since most of his knowledge of the world comes from his reading of romantic novels, he can be amusing and exasperating at the same time. He's amusing when he shows his imperfect understanding of what he has read, and when he gives literal meaning to things that existed only in the imagination of the people who wrote those books. He's exasperating when books lead him to ignore the real world he lives in, especially when he forgets the people around him and allows his fantasies to affect their lives.

Huck is as ambivalent about Tom as he is about himself. On the one hand, Huck idolizes him. He sees Tom's wide reading and vivid imagination as qualities that set Tom far above himself, and he often mentions how Tom would have enjoyed some particularly difficult feat that he himself has just pulled off.

On the other hand, Huck has little patience with fantasies, including Tom's. Huck is interested in the concrete, the here-and-now, and he doesn't have the faith necessary to engage in fantasies. He often becomes annoyed with Tom's daydreams, but he always goes along because he believes that Tom is one of his betters.

Other Elements

SETTING

The setting of *Huckleberry Finn*— a relatively short southern stretch of the Mississippi River—is an area that Mark Twain knew as well as anyplace on earth. It includes not only his home town of Hannibal, Missouri, fictionalized as St. Petersburg, but the river he loved as a boy and came to revere during his days as a riverboat pilot.

Many people have said that the river is a character in the novel, a living, powerful, even godlike force that has as much to do with what happens to Huck as any of the human characters he meets during the story. Huck himself encourages this kind of comment, since he reserves his most touching language for his descriptions of the river. Even after a flood, even after a river accident that nearly destroys the raft, Huck never has an unkind word to say about this "character."

But the river makes up only part of the book's setting. There are also all those towns and villages that

Huck visits, and the people who live in them. These limbs of civilization on the body of the river give Huck—and Twain, of course—a chance to observe and comment on 19th-century American society.

If Twain becomes poetic when he's writing about the river, he can be vitriolic about the people who live near it. Neither of these extremes alone would have resulted in a very satisfactory novel, but Twain is successful in playing one against the other. He can rail at the human race and sing hymns to one of nature's greatest creations, and he can do it because of the shifting setting, because Huck goes from river to town and back again throughout the novel.

THEMES

"What is the book about?" can be a tricky question. The plot of almost any novel can be summarized in a few sentences, but those sentences might tell very little about what goes on in the book.

Most good books are about dozens of things—plot, several characters, general setting, specific scenes, dialogue, symbols, description, implication, and on and on. And when you get to talking about a book that has been read and loved for more than a century, it's almost impossible to nail down exactly what it's about. Still, there are some general statements that can be made about the book, each of them at least partially true.

It's possible to read *Huckleberry Finn* with only one of these statments in mind and still get a lot out of it. But your reading will be more satisfying if you can keep them all in mind. After you've read the novel, you can decide for yourself which of them come closest to saying what *Huck Finn* is really about.

Here are some general statements about *Huck Finn:*

1. *Huck Finn* is an adventure book about the escapades of a boy who has run away from home. The main character is candid, trustworthy, and funny, and he offers us a boy's-eye view of the interesting characters he meets during his trip.

2. *Huck Finn* is a novel about growing up. Huck not only runs away from his father, he also undertakes to make it on his own. Before he can, he has to go through certain rites of passage, which will allow him to enter the adult world. Helping a slave to escape is one of these rites, since it forces Huck to make decisions about right and wrong, decisions that will determine the kind of adult he will be.

3. *Huck Finn* is a satire of the American South in the 19th century. Slavery is its main target, but it attacks many human traits and institutions. As likable as he is, even Huck is the object of satire, especially his attitude toward blacks.

4. *Huck Finn* is an allegory about God and man. The Mississippi River is a god that provides both beauty and terror. Huck represents mankind's need to retreat (at least from time to time) from the real world and to take solace in the pleasures of religion.

5. *Huck Finn* is an allegory about good and evil. Huck represents the forces of good, and most of the people he meets represent evil. Although he doesn't win all his battles against evil, he never gives in to it. The ending of the book is a pessimistic statement about man's ability to overcome evil.

STYLE AND POINT OF VIEW

When novelist Ernest Hemingway said that all modern American literature stems from *Huckleberry Finn*, among the things he had in mind were Mark Twain's writing style and the point of view of the novel. If you were to read some of the books published in and around 1882, you'd see that Twain's novel could be classified as revolutionary.

In his time, most novels were a form of uplifting entertainment, light reading that would do no harm and might even do their readers some good. They were written with a prim, well-behaved audience in mind, an audience that expected to read about people like themselves, and that was most comfortable reading the language they themselves used in public.

Even before *Huckleberry Finn*, Twain never identified with such people. As a comic writer and lecturer, he often made fun of them, though he did it without alienating them and in a way that made them laugh. His language was never vulgar, but he avoided the fancy literary language expected of writers in his day.

In *Huckleberry Finn*, he introduced a character who was very unlike his readers, and he had him speak in a way that probably would have offended the ears of many people. In choosing Huck as his narrator, Twain was locking his novel into an unschooled, colloquial dialect.

Other writers had used regional dialects before Mark Twain, and he had written stories himself in which characters didn't speak the kind of English taught in schools. But with *Huckleberry Finn*, he introduced readers to a likable main character who spoke like someone they might meet in the street, but not at a church social.

The word likable is important. It's one of the things

that makes Huck unique for his time, as fictional characters go. Huck's story falls into the general classification of *picaresque* novels—stories in which we follow a central character through a series of adventures that may or may not cause him to change.

Probably the closest thing we have these days to picaresque novels is a certain kind of weekly TV series. Think of the action-adventure series in which a main character survives by his wits, usually engaging in violence and often breaking the law to get things done. In a series like that, the main character may be admirable because of his bravery or strength or quick thinking, but he isn't usually the kind of person parents want their kids to emulate.

For more than two centuries before Huck Finn came on the scene, picaresque heroes had played a large part in the popularization of the novel.

They were often thieves or murderers, though sometimes only liars and cheats. They rarely had any of the traditional virtues, and it's usually easy to see how the world would be better off without them. They might have been interesting, but they were rarely admirable.

With Huck, Twain broke this mold and started something new. He gave his readers a picaresque hero they couldn't fail to like. By making this character the narrator, Twain put him in the center of all the action, forcing us not only to see things through Huck's eyes, but to hear it all expressed through his language.

In this way, the language and the point of view are at least as important to the novel as anything that happens to Huck. And both may be even more important in the effect they have had on the novelists that followed Twain—on "all modern American literature," as Hemingway said.

FORM AND STRUCTURE

As with any published work, *Huckleberry Finn* has had its critics. Some people have said, for example, that Twain has Huck say certain things that no uneducated kid could ever have thought of. Others have said that some of the comic scenes in the novel are badly placed, coming immediately after tragic events.

But it's on the subject of structure that most criticisms of the book are made. Even among readers who like the book, a large portion will admit that they were disappointed with the last quarter—the section in which Tom Sawyer puts Jim and Huck through his meaningless "adventure" rituals.

Up until that point, the book has a pretty tight structure; and then, some people say, it wanders off into another story that has little to do with everything that went before. Not everyone agrees with this criticism. Before you decide whether or not you do, think about the structure of the novel.

The story divides pretty neatly into three sections. In the first section, Huck introduces himself, Tom, and Jim (briefly). He gives us a lot of information about what he thinks and how he's different from the people he knows. And we learn more about him by contrasting him with Tom. We also get a good serving of humor in the salty comments he makes about such people as Miss Watson. This section ends when Huck fakes his own murder and runs away.

The second—and longest—section has Huck running away from civilization and Jim running away from slavery. We meet Jim as a human being in this section, and learn a good deal more about what makes Huck tick. We get a pleasant view of life on the river, and a dim view of human nature. This is the section in which we come to understand why Huck wants to get away from the civilized world. The section ends when he goes to Uncle Silas' farm to find Jim.

In the final section, Huck is back in civilized society, so solidly that he's living with Tom Sawyer's relatives. Once Tom shows up, the rest of the book is more about him than Huck or Jim. Jim becomes little more than a stage prop, and Huck is an observer, as Tom once again steals center stage.

Is that last section out of place in the novel, as some people charge? After winning our sympathy for Jim, did Twain make a mistake in letting Tom treat him like a piece of furniture, and in letting Huck go along just because of Tom's forceful personality?

Or did Twain have a good reason for including that long third section? Some writers have said he did. One of the explanations they offer is that Twain wanted to give Huck a chance actually to walk out on civilized society. To make that possible, Twain had to get Huck back into the world, and to show how that world contrasted with the one Huck was looking for.

Another explanation says that Twain brought Tom back into the story so that he could remove Huck from the limelight. Without Tom's shenanigans, Huck's real adventures, and all the good qualities they illustrated, would have made him a hero. And that's something he never could have dealt with. To keep Huck from having to face such a thing, these writers say, Twain included the Tom Sawyer chapters and allowed Huck to slip away quietly at the end.

You may agree that the last quarter of the novel seems thoughtlessly tacked on; or you may accept one of the explanations you've just read. A third possibility is that you have your own ideas on why the final section of the novel does or doesn't fit in with what comes before it.

In any case, the structure of *Huck Finn* is a topic on which many serious readers disagree. Whichever side of the debate you take, just be sure you have defensible reasons for it.

The Story

CHAPTER 1

In the opening paragraph, Huck introduces himself to us as the narrator of the story. He talks to us in a relaxed, matter-of-fact tone that makes him sound friendly, honest, and maybe a little less respectful than he should be. He does, after all, come close to calling Mark Twain a liar.

Try to imagine Twain writing that paragraph, in which he has a fictional character accuse him of "stretching the truth" in an earlier book. Twain seems to be sharing a joke with you, the reader, but Huck isn't in on the joke. Huck doesn't say it to be funny. He says it innocently, not realizing that it could be taken as an insult.

Keep this trick of Twain's in mind as you read the book, because you'll find him doing it dozens of times. He'll be expecting you to understand things better than Huck, who's just a simple, almost illiterate kid. Twain will often be winking at you over Huck's head, the way two grownups might be quietly amused at the naïve things said by a young child.

Huck tells us that he's been living with the Widow Douglas, a woman he seems to like even though she has set out to "sivilize" him. His friend, Tom Sawyer, has persuaded him to go along with her, and Huck finds himself living in a house, wearing clean clothes, and eating meals on schedule—activities that seem very unnatural to him.

Although he's able to put up with the widow, her sister, Miss Watson, is another story. He describes her as a "slim old maid, with goggles on," and he complains about her trying to teach him spelling and manners. When she tells him about heaven and hell, he figures hell must be a better place, since Miss Watson assures him that she is going to heaven.

After an unpleasant session with Miss Watson, Huck goes up to his room and stares out the window. The night sounds of the woods make him sad, until one sound begins to stand out—he recognizes it as a signal from Tom Sawyer. Huck sneaks out of the house, feeling better now that he and his friend are off on an adventure.

CHAPTER 2

As Huck and Tom begin sneaking past the house in the dark, they make enough noise to attract the attention of Jim, Miss Watson's black slave. He comes out of the kitchen to see what caused the noise, sits down in the dark to wait for it to happen again, and falls asleep.

Tom slips into the kitchen to steal some candles for their adventure, and when he comes back, Huck is anxious to get going. But Tom insists on playing a prank on Jim before they leave. Huck knows this is a dumb idea, because if Jim wakes up, they'll be in deep trouble for sneaking out of the house after dark.

But dumb or not, Tom gets to do what he wants. As the self-appointed leader of the gang, Tom manages to get his own way just about all the time. So he lifts Jim's hat from his head and hangs it on a nearby limb.

Huck tells us that Jim later turned this incident into an elaborate tale of being visited by witches while he slept.

Huck and Tom get together with the rest of the gang, and they all travel downriver to a cave Tom has picked out as a meeting place. Huck reports what happens at the meeting, making no comment on it.

At the meeting, Tom outlines his plan for forming a gang of bloodthirsty robbers. He talks of the blood oath they'll take together. He says that anyone who reveals the gang's secrets will be killed, along with his whole family. He describes what will be done with the body of such a traitor.

Where does Tom get such ideas? He gets them from the adventure books he reads. Unfortunately, he doesn't always understand what he's reading, as you'll be able to tell later from his explanation of what it means to "ransom" someone.

Read this whole scene very carefully, and you'll get a good picture of what Tom is—a kid who's smarter than most of the others, but not nearly as smart as he thinks he is. Tom *does* read more than the others, he *does* have a quick mind and a lively imagination. But he's the leader of this group more because of his forceful personality than any real difference between him and the others. If you wanted to be very critical of Tom, you could call him two things—a phony and a bully.

But Huck doesn't say anything along these lines. He doesn't see how ridiculous Tom's statements are. He works from the assumption that Tom is much smarter than he is and he takes Tom's statements at face value. As was true in the first chapter, Twain doesn't expect you to be that naïve. He expects you to see the truth about Tom, even if the young narrator misses it.

CHAPTER 3

The morning after the secret meeting, Huck has to put up with a scolding from Miss Watson and—worse—looks of hurt disappointment from the Widow Douglas. Miss Watson tells him he might get better if he prays, but he has his doubts about that.

Huck then tells us about a time when he went off into the woods and "had a long think" about praying. (He's in the habit of going off by himself and thinking when something bothers him.) If prayer is so powerful, he wonders, why don't people like the Deacon, Widow Douglas, and Miss Watson have everything they want?

The widow explains to him that praying will win him "spiritual gifts," and that the best kind of prayer is the kind that's meant to help other people. Huck goes off and thinks about that for a while, then decides that he isn't interested in something that will help other people but not him.

Huck also talks about the difference between the Providence (God) that the widow tells him about, and the one he hears about from Miss Watson. Huck thinks they are two different Gods, and this is another case of Twain talking to you over the head of his narrator. Twain is suggesting that God can be imagined in different ways by people with different personalities.

Huck says he'd prefer belonging to the widow's God, but he can't see why God would want someone so ignorant, low-down, and ornery. By this time you should begin to see that Twain doesn't share Huck's low opinion of himself—and he doesn't expect you to share it either.

Huck believes that just about everyone he comes in contact with is better than he is. For example, as much as he dislikes Miss Watson, he doesn't immediately dismiss everything she tells him. He may reject it after he's thought it over a bit, but his first reaction is, "She's smarter than I am. Maybe she's right."

He even goes along with everything Tom Sawyer suggests, no matter how silly the suggestion is. Tom reads books and goes to school. Tom is "sivilized," so he must be better than Huck.

At this point, Huck talks a bit about his father, who disappeared more than a year ago. Pap was a drunkard who used to beat Huck whenever he was sober. Huck certainly doesn't miss him. He tells us that a body was found floating in the river, and that some people believe it was Pap. Huck doesn't think so, and he's afraid his father will show up again.

Huck isn't very excited about playing robber with Tom's gang. They do a lot of running around, he tells us, and they scare people sometimes, but they aren't stealing anything. And they certainly haven't killed anybody yet.

In Tom's imagination, though, they *are* doing all the things he said they would. They have swords and guns, they steal jewels and gold ingots, they're getting ready to ambush "a whole parcel of Spanish merchants and rich Arabs."

Huck knows they're really brandishing broomsticks and stealing turnips, but Tom's description of the Spaniards and "A-rabs," with their elephants and camels, does catch his interest. So he shows up the next day to take part in the spectacle.

What Huck sees is a Sunday School picnic for little kids. What Tom sees are the Spaniards and Arabs he described. The gang has been enchanted by magicians, Tom explains, and they only *think* they're looking at a kid's picnic.

Read this conversation between Huck and Tom

carefully, because it shows a contrast between the two boys—a contrast that will become important later in the book. In this conversation, Huck makes several suggestions about how they can carry out their plan to rob and kill. Tom counters all of Huck's suggestions with fantasy elements from the books he's read—magicians, magic lamps, giant genies.

Huck is thinking about the concrete world around him; Tom is following a set of "rules" he's put together from his books. The two boys are not talking about the same thing.

Tom becomes exasperated with Huck's realistic, down-to-earth approach to robbing and killing, and finally calls him a "perfect saphead" for not knowing anything. Huck, of course, doesn't claim that he isn't a saphead, because he secretly believes he is. Instead of arguing, he goes off to test what Tom has said. He tries conjuring up a giant by rubbing a tin lamp.

When nothing happens, he puts Tom into the same class as the widow and Miss Watson. Tom might believe that the stuff he reads about is true; but to Huck, it has "all the marks of a Sunday school."

CHAPTER 4

In the first three chapters Twain established the personality of his main character. In this chapter he begins to develop the plot—a series of "adventures" involving Huck.

Each of these adventures is almost a story in itself, even though most of them go on for several chapters. So from here on it would probably be better to read the book in sections instead of one chapter at a time. I'll still summarize the novel chapter by chapter, but I'll let you know when a new section begins and how many chapters it invovles.

You should read Chapters 4–7 as a unit, since they all deal with Pap, Huck's alcoholic father. Huck begins Chapter 4 by telling us he has actually adjusted to civilized life. The first paragraph suggests that he doesn't know as much arithmetic as he thinks he does, but he doesn't "take no stock in mathematics, anyway."

He isn't deliriously happy with school, and living in a house, and all the rest of it, but he doesn't hate it the way he used to. Then one morning he knocks over the salt shaker at the breakfast table.

As we saw near the end of Chapter 1, Huck is very superstitious and gets himself quite worked up over signs of bad luck. He's certain the spilled salt means something terrible. Sure enough, when he goes outside, he sees bootprints in the snow, and he recognizes them as belonging to his father.

What he instantly does might seem puzzling at first, but we get an explanation soon enough. He runs to Judge Thatcher, who is the trustee of the money Huck got for helping to catch a gang of robbers. (That adventure is mentioned in the second paragraph of the novel.)

He begs the judge to take the $6000 and the interest, so he "won't have to tell no lies." The judge doesn't really understand Huck's motives, but he buys the account from the boy for one dollar. Huck knows that his father is going to be after the money, and his father has beaten him in the past for less reason than $6000. He wants to be able to say he has no money—and he wants it to be the truth.

This shows us something interesting about Huck's character. Pap is not one of the people he respects. He's already told us he hopes never to see him again. He expects the man to beat him and to try to steal his money. *Yet, he's unwilling to tell a lie, even in such a desperate situation.* Remember, this is the boy who has told us how low-down and ornery he must be in the eyes of God.

After Huck gets rid of his money, he goes to visit Jim, Miss Watson's slave. Jim has a hair-ball that is supposed to have come from the stomach of an ox, and they both believe it has magical powers.

Huck asks Jim to use the hair-ball to predict what Pap is planning to do. Jim goes through a long, sing-song speech, in which he predicts so many things that he actually predicts nothing. He gets so carried away that he predicts things that will happen to Huck many years in the future.

Huck then goes up to his room and finds Pap waiting there for him.

NOTE: This is Jim's second appearance in the story, and very soon he will become a major character. This is as good a time as any to deal with the kind of person he is and with Twain's use of the word nigger.

In recent years, *The Adventures of Huckleberry Finn* has often been the subject of debate and has even been banned in some schools and public libraries. The argument and the censorship revolve around the character of Jim.

Jim is illiterate, superstitious, childlike, easily led, and apparently not very bright. Some people think the book could lead readers—especially young readers—to conclude that this is what all black people are like.

The same people may be offended by Huck's use of the word nigger to refer to Jim. To us in the 20th century, nigger is an ugly word that many people would like to see erased from the language.

On the other side of the argument are people who point out that the novel is set in a southern state in the middle of the last century. In that setting, these people say, the word nigger had no special meaning, good or bad. It was simply a regional pronunciation of negro. These same people would say that, in the same setting, a character like Jim was much more typical than he would be today.

Whichever side of this argument you take, try to keep two things in mind. First, a novel can be good or bad regardless of how much it reflects your own view of the world. And second, as we've already seen, there's often a big difference between what Huck says and what Mark Twain believes.

CHAPTER 5

Huck's meeting with his father turns out not to be as bad as he had feared. Once he gets over the initial shock, Huck finds that he isn't scared of Pap at all. Instead of the terrifying creature he grew up with, Huck sees a pitiful old man who has worn his body down to a sickly mess.

What Pap sees is an "uppity" kid who has forgotten his place in society. He rails at the boy for wearing clean clothes, for going to school, and mostly for having learned to read and write. Pap talks about illiteracy as though it's a mark of family pride, and he's outraged that Huck would try to be better than his father.

Then he asks for the money. Huck tells him the truth, and when he finally accepts it, Pap says he'll go to Judge Thatcher. Of course he can't get the money, because the deal Huck made with the judge was completely legal.

Pap does win one legal battle, though. Judge Thatcher and Widow Douglas go to court to have Huck taken from his father and placed in their care. The judge in the case, a new man in town, rules against them, even though he knows their intentions are good.

This same judge then decides to reform Pap by inviting him to stay at his house. After supper, Pap announces that he will never drink again, and he and the judge cry and carry on about the new life Pap is going to lead.

That night, Pap sneaks out of the judge's house, sells the coat the judge gave him, and spends the money on liquor. They find him the next morning sleeping on the ground, dead drunk, with a broken arm.

The judge was probably the only person in town who was surprised.

CHAPTER 6

Once Pap regains control of himself, he hires a lawyer to sue Judge Thatcher for the money that once belonged to Huck. Although he occasionally catches Huck and beats him for going to school, Huck continues to go, to spite his father. Then one day Pap kidnaps his son and brings him to a log cabin on the Illinois shore, on the other side of the river.

Whenever he's away, Pap keeps Huck locked in the cabin. But when his father is there, they fish and hunt or just hang around doing not much of anything. Except for the imprisonment, Huck finds he likes getting back to his old style of living, and he doesn't want to go back to the widow's home any more.

The trouble is, he can't stay with Pap, either. His father beats him more and more, until Huck decides to work out an escape plan. He finds a saw and cuts a hole in the cabin wall, then covers it up to wait for a chance to get out, while his father is away.

Soon after this, Pap comes back from town in a terrible mood. He starts drinking and complaining about the courts, the widow, and a number of other things. After a few drinks, he goes into a long speech about the government. This speech is important in at least one way—it shows how Twain felt about racial bigotry.

Pap complains about not getting justice from his government, when he has had all the anxiety and expense of raising a son. We know, however, that this isn't true, that Pap has been about as bad a father as anyone can imagine. We know that he isn't the good citizen he claims to be. And we know that his threat to leave the country is laughable, considering what an undesirable character he is.

As he does with Huck, Twain is talking over Pap's head to the reader, and we know how Twain wants us to feel. The same thing is true in the second part of Pap's harangue, in which he berates the government for allowing a black college professor to vote right along with a white man like himself. Twain makes Pap look ridiculous for suggesting that he is superior to the professor, simply because he's white.

Huck listens to all this, waiting for Pap to fall asleep so he can slip out of the cabin. Unfortunately, Pap has a restless night and never completely falls asleep. He has a nightmare, in which he fights off the angel of death. Then he confuses Huck with the angel and starts attacking him. When he finally falls asleep,

Huck takes the rifle from the wall and loads it. He sits there quietly, hoping his father won't attack him again.

CHAPTER 7

When Pap wakes up, he doesn't remember anything about attacking Huck as the angel of death, and he wants to know why Huck is asleep in a chair with the rifle in his lap. Huck is afraid he won't believe the truth, so he says that somebody tried to break in during the night.

You remember that Huck gave away more than $6000 to avoid having to tell a lie to his father. How can he lie so easily in this situation? Later in the book, Huck himself will give you an answer to that question. In the meantime, think about whether you see any difference between the lie he refused to tell and this one.

While he's out getting some fish for breakfast, Huck sees an abandoned canoe drifting by. He wades out and gets the canoe and hides it in the woods. An escape plan is beginning to form in his head. He's glad he lied to Pap about somebody trying to break in, because that lie will help him in his plan.

After dinner, Pap goes to town to sell some logs. Huck is sure he won't be back until morning, which will give him plenty of time to put his escape plan into effect.

Read the description of Huck's escape carefully. It's a pretty elaborate plan, worked out to the smallest detail, obviously the work of a bright kid. In the middle of his description, Huck says he wishes Tom Sawyer were with him to "throw in the fancy touches." When you read it, you'll see that this plan doesn't need the kind of fancy touches Tom would add. It's complete as it is, and unlike Tom's make-believe adventures, this escape is the real thing.

The plan is intended to make everyone think Huck was murdered. This is important to him, since he isn't running away only from his father. He's running from Judge Thatcher, too, and the Widow Douglas, and all the other people he knows. He's determined to set out on his own and to leave behind his whole life up until this night.

As long as no one is looking for a living Huck, he figures he can stop anywhere he wants to take time to make further plans. He decides on nearby Jackson's Island as his temporary hideout. Then, satisfied with the ways things are working, he lies down in the canoe and falls asleep.

When he wakes up, he hears someone rowing toward his island, and he soon discovers it's Pap, coming back earlier than Huck expected. He unhitches the canoe and floats downstream as quietly as possible.

Something happens at this point in the narration that you should pay special attention to. It will happen again and again throughout the book, and you'll want to recognize it when it does.

What happens is that Huck describes what it's like on the river. It begins with "The sky looks ever so deep. . . ." Whenever Huck talks about living on the river, his tone of voice changes. His language becomes gentler and less harsh than usual. Sometimes he becomes almost poetic.

Imagine a friend talking to you about a date, or about sports, or cars, or any subject you both have in common. Then suppose the friend suddenly shifted to talking about a much-loved baby brother. Think of the probable contrast in your friend's language and tone of voice.

Huck loves the Mississippi River the way most of us love people. If you want to know how much Mark Twain loved the river, read *Life on the Mississippi* some time. For now, you can get some idea of Twain's feeling by paying close attention to Huck's descriptions, beginning with the short, affectionate one we get in this chapter.

Huck gets to Jackson's Island just before daybreak. He hides his canoe in some willow branches, then lies down to take a nap before breakfast.

CHAPTER 8

Huck wakes after daybreak "feeling rested and ruther comfortable and satisfied." He seems to have forgotten last night's harrowing experience, and he lies in the grass enjoying the sun, the trees, and a couple of friendly-looking squirrels. He feels completely at home.

He's torn from this pleasant state by the sound of cannon fire. He gets up to see a ferry boat moving toward the island. He knows it's filled with people searching the water for his dead body.

From a hiding place at the shore, Huck watches as the ferry comes so close to the island that he can almost reach out and touch the people on it. He sees his father, Tom Sawyer, the widow, the judge—almost everybody he knows is on that ferry searching for him. He looks into those familiar faces, and he doesn't make a sound.

NOTE: If you ever considered running away from home when you were young, you might want to think about this scene for a minute. A lot of kids fantasize about doing it, and the fantasy often involves grief-stricken relatives and friends. Fortunately, most people never do run away from home, because they decide they need those relatives and friends more than they need freedom.

Huck is hiding on the island, having successfully fooled everyone he knows into thinking he's dead. Now he comes face to face with all those people. Imagine yourself in that situation. Most of us would probably abandon the idea of running, and yell out, "Here I am! I'm not really dead!"

That would seem to be the natural response if you were suddenly confronted by everyone who's close to you. But it isn't Huck's response. He just crouches there silently, letting everyone in his life float by.

You can look at this incident in a number of ways. Maybe it shows that Huck is so much in control of his emotions that he doesn't do the "natural" thing. Maybe it shows that none of these people really means anything to him, in spite of what he's told us. Or it might show that he doesn't understand how sorrowful some of those people are. Since he doesn't think much of himself, he'd find it hard to believe that someone else thinks much of him.

All these interpretations are possible, as well as some others that may occur to you. Even if you aren't ready to interpret the incident in one particular way, keep it in mind as you read on. You'll learn other things about Huck, and you may be able to interpret this better later on.

Once the ferry is gone, Huck is overcome by loneliness. He listens to the river and watches the stars for a while, then decides to go to sleep. "There ain't no better way to put in time when you are lonesome," he says. He sounds as though he's had this problem before.

After three days on the island, Huck makes a terrifying discovery. The remains of a campfire tell him that he isn't alone. As frightened as he is, he decides that he has to find out who the other person is. After a long search, he finds himself back at the campfire. This time there's a man sleeping near it.

He waits quietly until the man wakes up and throws the blanket off his face. When Huck sees that it's Miss Watson's slave, Jim, he skips from his hiding place to say hello.

It takes him a while to convince Jim that he isn't seeing a ghost. He explains how he created the illusion that he was dead, and Jim says it was a hoax worthy of Tom Sawyer himself. Then Huck asks Jim why he's on the island.

Jim first makes him promise not to tell anyone. When Huck promises, Jim confesses that he has run away from Miss Watson.

Notice Huck's shocked reaction to this news. Remember that he grew up with people who believed that stealing a slave was as serious as committing murder. A modern equivalent of a runaway slave might be someone who murders a police officer.

Huck's shock is an expression of this belief. He's never heard anyone question the institution of slavery, and he has every reason to believe that Jim has done something terrible.

All of this makes the next part of the conversation interesting. Jim reminds Huck that he promised not to tell. Without hesitating, Huck says he'll keep his word. He realizes that "people would call me a low-down Abolitionist and despise me for keeping mum." And he really believes those people would be right. But he'll keep his word. "I ain't a-going back there, anyways," he explains.

Not turning Jim in is a monumental decision for Huck to make, even though he makes it on the spot. This is not just a boy running away from home. It's someone who has decided to turn his back on everything "home" stands for, even one of its most cherished beliefs.

The rest of the chapter includes three things you may find interesting. First, Jim explains why he's running away and how he got to the island. Then he does what might qualify as a comedy monologue on things that foreshadow bad luck.

The last part of the chapter might remind you of comedy teams in which one person provides all the straight lines and the other does all the jokes. Jim tells a long story about a time when he had some money. The routine ends with a punch line that might give you a clue to how Twain felt about slavery when he wrote this book.

CHAPTER 9

Neither Huck nor Jim has any intention of going back to the village; so, without actually stating it, they've decided to be outcasts together. This chapter shows them starting out on their new life.

Huck leads Jim to a cavern he found while he was exploring the island. Jim convinces him that they should carry all their gear up to this place because there are going to be heavy rains. Huck doesn't like having to do all that work, but he decides to go along.

Sure enough, the rain begins right after dinner. Huck gives another of his "poetic" descriptions when he tells about the rain. He seems to be perfectly satisfied with his new life.

It rains for so many days that the river floods. Huck and Jim take the canoe out from time to time to see what they can find. On one of their trips, they retrieve a 12 x 16-foot raft, well-built and sturdy. They bring it back to the island for possible use later.

On another outing, they climb into the window of a two-story house that's floating by. In one room they find the body of a man who has been shot in the back. Jim covers the man's face to keep Huck from seeing it. Jim's behavior might be a little puzzling here, but it will be explained later. He seems to be trying to keep Huck away from the body. Huck, however, isn't much interested in seeing it.

They ransack the house for equipment and supplies they may need. Then they go back to the security of their island.

CHAPTER 10

The next morning Huck wonders aloud how the dead man was killed. Jim says it would be bad luck to talk about it. He adds that unburied corpses are more likely to haunt people than buried ones. That sounds reasonable to Huck, so he drops the subject.

Most of this chapter is about bad luck and its causes. As you read it, you should be able to detect Mark Twain in the background, having a laugh over some of the superstitions he believed when he was a boy.

Huck tells us that after he handled some snakeskin, Jim warned him that bad luck was coming. Sure enough, three days later Jim is bitten by a rattlesnake because of something Huck has done.

Even though Huck is directly responsible for what happens to Jim, he counts this as the bad luck that Jim predicted. Twain is probably making a small joke here about how superstitious people will go out of their way to find things that make their superstitions seem true.

But he's also setting us up for another joke on the same topic. Huck tells us a story about Hank Bunker, who waited a full *two years* before his bad luck finally showed up. The funniest part of the story is the description of what happened to the man and how he was buried.

NOTE: The subject of good and bad luck comes up often in Huck's narration, and you might have suspected by now that it's more than simply a way for Twain to get some laughs. Jim's attitude toward the supernatural, for example, should tell you something about his self-image and about his view of the world.

Maybe you remember a conversation the two had when they first met on the island in Chapter 8. Huck asked Jim why he never talked about signs of good luck, why he dwelt so much on bad omens. Jim's response was that, first, there are very few signs of good luck; and second, that good luck wasn't the sort of thing you had to know about in advance.

To Jim, the world is an endlessly threatening place. Danger is hiding behind every tree and under every rock. At any moment, everything you have could be taken away from you by forces over which you have no control.

If you can imagine growing up as a slave in 19th-century America, you can understand how Jim could have developed such a view of life. A slave had no status as a human being; he could be beaten or even killed by a master; he was a piece of property who could be sold on a whim, even if that meant permanent separation from his own family.

To someone who grew up under conditions like these, dark and unexplained forces could become a part of everyday life. But how about Huck? Does the same explanation hold true for him?

It's true that Huck has had his share of hardship; you don't have to look any farther than Pap. To a kid, the unpredictable behavior of a cruel, drunken father is no less frightening than the things a slave had to worry about all the time.

That unwarranted and unpredictable cruelty could help to explain why Huck has such a low opinion of himself. If his own father treats him like a piece of dirt, he probably finds it easy to believe that he *is* a piece of dirt. And if his own father could turn on him in an instant and suddenly start beating him, Huck might find it easy to believe that the world is filled with unexplained forces that could ruin his life just as suddenly.

Still, there are at least two differences between Jim and Huck. One is that Huck is white. No matter how badly he thinks of himself, somewhere, deep inside, he knows that there's at least a chance that he could be a respectable person some day. For Jim, that would be inconceivable.

A second difference is that Huck is a boy, on his way to becoming an adult. He's also inclined to examine ideas before accepting or rejecting them. So he asks a lot of questions about the omens that Jim believes with all his heart.

In most cases Huck ends up accepting what Jim tells him. But that doesn't mean he always will. He still has the potential of learning and of outgrowing things he now believes. As you read on, you'll see some of this taking place.

The chapter ends with Huck dressing up as a girl so he can go to town and find out the latest news about him and Jim. He puts on a dress and a bonnet that they took from the floating house the night before. After paddling the canoe to the mainland, he finds himself outside the house of someone who has just moved into town.

CHAPTER 11

In this chapter the question of lying will come up again. You remember that Huck gave up $6000 to avoid having to tell his father a lie. In this chapter you'll see him concoct tales about himself with all the confidence of an experienced artist painting a portrait.

He not only has no qualms about telling such lies, he seems to enjoy it (and he's very good at it, besides). As you read the chapter, think about his apparently contradictory attitude toward telling the truth.

He goes into the woman's house and presents himself as a girl on her way to her uncle's house at the other end of town. He gets the woman to talking, and when she finally gets around to the stuff that matters, he learns that Pap has disappeared and that Jim is a prime suspect in Huck's murder. Worse than that, the woman has seen campfire smoke on Jackson's Island. Her husband is planning to go there with a friend late that night to hunt for the runaway slave and collect the reward.

In his nervousness over hearing this news, Huck starts fooling with the woman's sewing equipment. She watches him try to thread a needle, and the way he does it makes her suspicious. She then comes up with two other "tests" for Huck, and the way he reacts convinces her she's talking to a boy, not a girl.

Has Huck's real identity been discovered? Huck is too quick witted to let that happen. He admits that the woman is right, but makes up a sad story about the terrible events that led him to try this disguise. The woman not only believes him; she offers him some advice on how to act more like a girl, and she prepares a snack for him to have on the rest of his trip. (You'll have to decide for yourself on the reliability of the woman's tests for the differences between males and females.)

As soon as Huck's out of the woman's sight, he races to the canoe and paddles back to the island. He stops first at the north end and lights a campfire to attract the men who will be looking for Jim. Then he goes to the south end and rouses Jim.

When Huck says "They're after us!," Jim acts quickly, without asking questions. They pack everything they own on the raft, push it out, and silently leave the island. Their long journey down the Mississippi River has begun.

CHAPTER 12

With this chapter, the main part of the book begins. Chapters 12 and 13 deal with Huck and Jim's first adventure while traveling along the Mississippi.

Huck begins by telling us that Jim built a wigwam on the raft so they could keep their things dry, and he even built a fire when it rained. (Keep in mind that the raft is 12 × 16 feet, about as big as a large bedroom in many modern houses.)

He gives us another of his quietly moving descriptions of living on the river, including a comment on seeing the city of St. Louis for the first time. He describes going ashore late each night to buy food and to "borrow" things they couldn't afford.

This section includes some interesting distinctions between stealing and borrowing. There's no doubt that Twain intended the distinctions to be funny; but they also remind us that Huck has a private set of moral standards. The standards may be unconventional, and sometimes laughable, but he does try to live up to them, and that's an important thing to remember.

Then comes the incident with the disabled steamboat, the *Walter Scott*. In using this name for a ship that was on the verge of sinking, Twain was probably making a small joke. Sir Walter Scott, author of *Ivanhoe* and other romantic novels, was a popular novelist in the 19th century. Twain often wrote scathing criticisms of such novels, believing that they were written by hacks who knew little about the real world and nothing about the people who live in it.

NOTE: Twain has Huck describe his search of the steamboat in some detail, and he uses a number of nautical terms you might find confusing. Here's a brief glossary that should make your reading a bit more enjoyable:

Texas   A shelter for officers on the upper deck, also called the texas deck

Pilot-house   An enclosed structure from which the ship is navigated

Derrick   A device for lifting cargo on or off the ship

Labboard *(larboard)*   The left side of the ship

Stabboard (starboard)   The right side

Guys   Ropes or cables

Skylight   The pilot-house roof, which can be opened and closed

---

Against Jim's wishes, they climb aboard the steamboat to see what they can find. When they hear voices, Jim races back to the raft, but Huck is too curious to leave without finding out what's going on.

The justification he uses is interesting: "Tom Sawyer wouldn't back out now." After all the things that have happened to Huck, and even now, in the midst of something really dangerous, he still sees himself as a follower of a boy who "holds up" Sunday School picnics and steals turnips.

When he finds out that the voices belong to three thieves, and that murder is part of their plan, Huck decides to get out. Jim gives him the bad news that the raft has broken loose, and the chapter ends with a cliffhanger.

CHAPTER 13

Huck knows that a steamboat always has a small boat—a skiff—that's used for taking one or two people ashore in shallow water, and he and Jim start looking for it. They almost lose their chance at the skiff, since two of the thieves plan on using it themselves; they mean to abandon the third to sink along with the steamboat.

But greed interrupts their escape, and the two thieves go back inside to get some money they've left behind. Huck and Jim get into the skiff, cut it loose, and silently slip away.

As soon as they're free, Huck begins to worry—not about himself and Jim, but about the three men they have left stranded. He thinks of "how dreadful it was, even for murderers, to be in such a fix," and he tells Jim he wants to go ashore and try to get some help for them.

They find the raft, load it with the thieves' loot from the skiff, and climb aboard. Then Huck arranges for a meeting place with Jim and rows the skiff to the shore.

The scene that follows is interesting in two respects. First, you'll see Huck once again proving himself a champion liar—or yarn spinner, as Twain probably would have preferred to think of him. In order to save the three criminals from almost certain drowning, he tells a ferryboat captain an elaborate tale about his family being stranded on the disabled steamboat.

The second thing to note about the scene is Huck's quick mind and his understanding of what makes people tick. Early in the conversation the captain makes a chance reference to someone named Jim Hornback. Huck is shrewd enough to figure out how the captain feels about Hornback, and he works the man's name into his plea for help.

When he leaves the captain, Huck feels better for having done what he could to help the men. "I wished the widow knowed about it," he says. "I judged she would be proud of me for helping these rapscallions, because rapscallions and dead-beats is the kind the widow and good people takes the most interest in."

What Huck is referring to here—without realizing it, of course—is the traditional Christian belief that sinners deserve more help than the rest of us. Several of the parables of Jesus in the New Testament make this point.

Huck doesn't understand why good people would be most interested in helping "rapscallions and dead-beats," but his instinctive urge to help such lowlife puts him much closer to at least one Christian ideal than almost everybody he comes across in this novel.

CHAPTER 14

Read Chapters 14 to 16 together and you'll see three important developments. First, the relationship between Huck and Jim begins to change, in a way that Huck would never have considered possible. Second,

Huck has serious doubts about the morality of helping a slave escape. And third, the two of them are separated by an accident on the river.

You might find several different layers of meaning in Chapter 14. I'll talk about two of them here.

The first level is the comic one. Huck and Jim have a conversation that's similar to dozens you've seen in movies and TV comedies, usually with comedy teams.

In this "classic" comedy situation, two characters are talking about a subject, and neither one knows very much about it. But one of the characters is the dominant one, in charge of the situation, maybe even the bully. The audience knows that they're both uninformed, and that's where the laughs come from. The dominant character always wins the argument, of course, but not because he or she really knows more.

If you aren't familiar with Laurel and Hardy or Abbott and Costello, you may remember Lucy and Ethel from the TV series "I Love Lucy." All three pairs of comedians used this kind of comedy routine, and earlier in the book Twain used it himself, when Tom Sawyer called Huck "a perfect saphead" for not understanding things. (He'll use it again, often.)

In this chapter Huck is the dominant character because he's white. He and Jim talk about the Old Testament story of King Solomon, who had a reputation for being wise. In the biblical story, two women came to him to settle a dispute over who is the real mother of the baby that one of them was carrying.

Solomon said there was no way to settle the dispute, and he ordered that the baby be cut in two, and one half be given to each woman. One woman said that was fine with her; the other was appalled at the suggestion and offered to give up her claim to allow the baby to live. Solomon concluded that the second woman was the real mother and gave the baby to her.

Jim contends that no really wise man would have suggested cutting a baby in two as a solution to a dispute. Huck tries to tell him he's missing the point, but Jim is adamant in contending that it was a stupid thing to do.

The outcome of the argument is the second level of meaning in the chapter. The important thing to notice is that *Huck gives in without winning the argument.* Huck is willing to lose an argument to a slave; and Jim dares to argue with a white person until he wins. Without realizing it, both characters have undergone a radical change in their attitudes, a change that would have shocked just about everyone they both knew.

The chapter ends with a second argument, which Jim also wins. This one shows Twain having some fun with one of his favorite targets—the French. He had a powerful bias against the French people, the French language, and—most of all—Americans who spoke French and wore French clothing to show how sophisticated they were. He gets in a little dig at these people at the end of Chapter 14.

One other point: showing off his superior knowledge, Huck tells Jim that the son of the French king is "the dolphin." The real word is *dauphin*, pronounced doe-FAN. It's only a small joke here, but the word will come up again later in the novel.

CHAPTER 15

Huck figures that they're now only three nights away from Cairo, Illinois, the point at which they'll be in a free state and Jim can stop running. The next night, though, they run into a heavy fog. Huck gets into the canoe to look for a place to tie the raft to, and he loses the raft.

What follows is another detailed description of the river; this one, though, is not touching, but frightening. Huck goes on for three full pages, telling us exactly what he did to try to get together with Jim in the fog, and it's easy to hear the experienced voice of Mark Twain, river pilot, in this passage.

When he finally does find the raft, Jim is sound asleep at the steering oar, and Huck decides to play a prank on him. He wakes Jim and pretends nothing has happened.

Jim figures he must have dreamed the whole thing, and he goes through an elaborate interpretation of what each detail symbolized. When he's finished, Huck shows him that it really did happen, and that he's just been the butt of a joke.

Jim's reaction to this is very emotional—and very daring for a slave who hasn't reached a free state yet. He says he was ready to die when he thought he'd lost Huck. He adds that anyone who would play such a prank on a friend is trash.

Try to imagine it. Try to reconstruct the relationship that existed between *all* white people and *all* black people in a Southern state in the middle of the 19th century. All his life, Jim has known that he could be hanged for talking to a white person—*any* white person—the way he has talked to Huck. As for Huck, all *his* life he's known that he has the right to have such a black person hanged.

But this knowledge doesn't stop Jim from saying what he feels, because he no longer thinks of Huck as a white person. He thinks of him as a friend.

Huck is a little less certain. "It was fifteen minutes,"

he tells us, "before I could work myself up to go and humble myself to a nigger."

But he does it. He apologizes to Jim who, at least for the moment, is his friend, and not a black man.

This apology sets the stage for the next chapter, when Huck makes an enormously important moral decision.

CHAPTER 16

As they get closer and closer to Cairo, both Huck and Jim begin getting fidgety. Jim's nervousness stems, of course, from his closeness to freedom, something he might never have dreamed of before his impulsive decision to run away.

Huck, however, is troubled by his gradual realization of exactly what he's doing. For the first time, he begins thinking about what it means to help a slave escape from his owner.

As we've seen in earlier chapters, Huck has a sense of right and wrong that would shame some of the people he refers to as his "betters." His conscience is now causing him a great deal of pain because he can't find an easy solution to his dilemma. Does he live up to the rules of the society he's been brought up in? Or does he do what seems to be the right thing for a friend?

When he hears Jim talk about getting an Abolitionist to help him steal his children—children that belong to someone Huck doesn't even know—Huck freezes with fear. At that point his conscience tells him to do the right thing—to turn the runaway slave in.

With the excuse that he's going to see how far they are from Cairo, Huck begins paddling the canoe to shore so he can tell the authorities about Jim. He loses some of his resolve, however, when his friend calls out that Huck is the only white gentleman who ever kept his promise to old Jim.

On his way to the shore he's stopped by two men looking for runaway slaves. He's now faced directly with the choice of "doing the right thing" or turning his friend in. He decides to do wrong. He tells the men he's traveling with a white man.

"I warn't man enough," he tells us. "Hadn't the spunk of a rabbit." It never occurs to him that what he's done might be considered the right thing. He has too low an opinion of himself to think that. Instead, he makes excuses for acting the way he did.

NOTE: Huck feels terrible for having done wrong. But if he had turned Jim in, he certainly wouldn't have felt any better. So why do right, he reasons, when it doesn't feel any better?

What he's trying to work out here is a conflict that everyone has to face many times in life. Do you live by the rules that someone else has taught you, even if they don't make much sense to you? Or do you follow your own conscience, even if all the people you know live by the rules they were taught? There's no question about which answer Twain favors. He has pitted slavery against friendship, and that stacks the deck in favor of individual conscience over the rules of society.

But the same conflict comes up in other situations, where the opposing forces aren't as clearcut as slavery versus friendship. In those situations it may be a lot harder to decide which action to take.

This is one of the reasons that some people disapprove of *The Adventures of Huckleberry Finn*, especially for young readers. They say that the book glorifies a lawbreaker by making him likable and by manipulating the audience into approving of what he does. This is the same criticism that is often leveled at movies like *The Godfather*, or TV shows in which police officers break the law in order to catch criminals.

So the larger moral question of conscience versus society's rules is one you'll have to work out for yourself, probably dozens of times. But in the context of the novel, there really isn't any question. Huck has done the right thing, no matter how strongly he insists that he's been bad.

As the chapter comes to an end, the raft is split in two by a carelessly piloted steamboat. The vivid description of what it was like to see that boat coming and to be on the raft when it hit is one of the best passages in the book. Read it slowly to get its full effect.

After he's been separated from Jim, Huck makes his way to shore. He finds himself surrounded by a pack of barking dogs, and he knows enough not to move.

CHAPTER 17

NOTE: The word *satire* is used in different ways. The dictionary gives more than one definition, and a whole list of synonyms. Without getting involved in any technical definitions, I'm going to use *satirize* to mean "making a comment on something by ridiculing it."

You've already seen Twain satirize such things as religion, superstition, and slavery, so you're familiar with the technique. The following episode, however, is the first in a series of extended satirical comments on the society that Twain—and Huck—grew up in.

In fact, some of these episodes are so extended that some critics have said they interfere with the flow of the novel, that Twain should have shortened them or left them out altogether. After you've read the whole book, you can decide on that for yourself. For now, be prepared to follow Huck on a series of visits ashore that lead to some pretty bitter comments on human nature. (The comments come not from Huck, but from Twain.) The first of these episodes is in Chapters 17 and 18, which you should read as a unit.

The barking dogs that surround Huck quiet down and back off at a command from inside the house. What follows is a series of suspicious questions and cautious instructions about moving slowly toward the house, all coming from a disembodied voice inside.

The people inside obviously think Huck is someone else. When he is finally let in, and the door immediately bolted behind him, he finds himself surrounded by men aiming pistols at him. They satisfy themselves that he isn't a Shepherdson, and their behavior immediately changes completely.

The Grangerfords become courteous, solicitous of his comfort, concerned about his welfare. They accept his story about being an orphan who fell overboard from a steamboat, and they not only feed him, but have him move in with Buck, a family member about his own age.

The suspicious behavior at their first meeting turns out to be the result of a decades-long feud between the Grangerfords and the Shepherdsons, but Huck quickly forgets this early treatment. Instead, he concentrates on what he sees as the marks of a fine, educated, aristocratic Southern family.

This is one of those scenes in which you can almost hear Mark Twain blowing a bugle to attract our attention from behind Huck's back. Twain grew up in a society that had a high regard for families like the Grangerfords. As an adult he came to feel contempt for people who used a family tree to hide inner decay.

Huck, being as simple as he is, will tell us about how everything looks on the surface. Twain wants us to look beyond what Huck is saying, to see more than he does.

For example, Huck describes in loving detail several of the decorations he finds in the Grangerfords' house. They're all in pretty poor taste, but Huck thinks they're just terrific.

The contrast is a little more obvious when Huck talks about the drawings left behind by young Emmeline Grangerford. They're dark and gloomy, as he tells us, but he doesn't realize how maudlin and sentimental they are. Read his description of what the family does to celebrate the dead girl's birthday each year, and see if you could have told it with a straight face as he does.

He does get in one good line about her when he says, "I reckoned that with her disposition she was having a better time in the graveyard." But he seems to be saying even this seriously, not for the laugh that it deserves.

If the drawings don't make Twain's point adequately, the poem drives it home with a sledgehammer. It's very difficult to read "Ode to Stephen Dowling Bots, Dec'd" without at least cracking a smile. (Dec'd is an abbreviation for deceased.)

The high-flown language is suitable for the passing of a president or a king. The subject matter is not only an insignificant boy, but one who came to an end in the manner of a cartoon character—by falling down a well. (The death of the boy isn't funny; the phrasing of it is, especially when the line is surrounded by the flowery language of the rest of the poem.)

Huck's final comment on this poem is, "If Emmeline Grangerford could make poetry like that before she was fourteen, there ain't no telling what she could 'a done by and by." Huck means it as a compliment. Twain is breathing a sigh of relief that something prevented her from going on, even if it had to be death itself.

The comments Huck makes after reading the poem are in the same vein—the admiration of a simple boy, which you aren't expected to take seriously. In this chapter Twain is poking gentle fun at the Grangerfords. He's setting us up for the bitter comment, which comes in the next chapter.

CHAPTER 18

"Col. Grangerford was a gentleman, you see. He was a gentleman all over; and so was his family."

Chapter 18 begins with this straightforward appraisal of the colonel by Huck. By the time you reach the end of the chapter, you'll see that Twain wrote those sentences with cutting sarcasm.

Huck's description of the colonel and some of his relatives is intended to show us how upright, how admirable, and how aristocratic the Grangerfords are. The colonel, for example, commands not only respect, but awe. He always walks straight, he's never frivolous or loud. He has all the characteristics of a being several cuts above the general run of the human race.

His family follows rigid rules of propriety. They have a dress code, and they carry themselves like aristocrats. Taken altogether, they're the most admirable people Huck has ever known.

But right after this description, he says something that might set an alarm going in the back of your mind. "Each person had their own nigger to wait on them," he tells us. (He adds that the slave assigned to him had an easy time, because Huck wasn't used to being waited on. But, of course, he would never conclude that this contrast hinted at some defect in the Grangerfords.)

Soon after he tells us how wonderful these people are, he recounts a conversation in which he asks Buck about the feud with the Shepherdsons. He asks a number of pointed questions, each of which makes the Grangerfords look pretty silly, but neither he nor Buck seems to see this.

From this conversation, he learns such things as these: it isn't clear exactly when the feud started; there may be no one left who remembers what the original argument was about; a large number of people from both families have been killed in the feud; many others have been injured; just this year Buck's fourteen-year-old cousin was killed; the boy chose to face his killer rather than be shot in the back while trying to get away; Buck thinks the Shepherdsons are brave and admirable men.

In giving us this conversation, what is Twain suggesting about these people? How intelligent can it be to continue a murderous feud whose origin has been forgotten? How admirable is a pride that allows family members to die for no apparent reason? What kind of people would teach their children to accept murder—and being murdered—as the normal course of events?

And finally, there is that admiration which Buck

has for the Shepherdsons. He expresses it so forcefully that it must be a part of the family creed along with all the rest of the nonsense.

This kind of respect for the enemy is what you might expect to find among opponents in sports. These people seem to think they're involved in a game. But it's a "game" in which their family members are dying.

The gentle fun that Twain seemed to be having in the previous chapter has by now turned to contempt. By the end of this chapter, even Huck is so disgusted by what he witnesses that he can't tell us about the details, for fear that he'll be as sick as he was when he saw them.

But even if their actions make him sick, Huck is still slow to learn the real lesson—that many of the people he looks up to are not as admirable as he thinks. Because a favor he did for one of the Grangerfords led to this latest outbreak of warfare, he holds himself responsible for the bloodshed. To Huck, the rules of his "betters" are still to be obeyed, even if those rules are supporting something as stupid as this feud. Huck also tells us in this chapter of how he gets back together with Jim, who has repaired the raft, which was damaged but not destroyed. Huck is very happy to get away from this particular branch of civilization, and he and Jim agree that "there warn't no home like a raft, after all."

CHAPTERS 19 AND 20

In these two chapters you'll meet the duke and the king, who will be with Huck longer than any other characters in the book, including Jim. In fact, until Chapter 30, Jim will practically disappear from the story.

As you read, you may find this puzzling. You may wonder where Jim is and what has happened to his escape to freedom. If so, you'll be in good company. Several critics have said that this is the weakest part of the novel, even though it contains some of the most interesting episodes.

There isn't any explanation for why Twain seems to have forgotten about Jim during this part of the story. The only argument some critics offer in Twain's defense is that the book is about Huck, not Jim. They say that leaving Jim for a long stretch isn't really a flaw in the novel, because Jim isn't the main character.

After you've finished the book, you can make up your mind about how important Jim's long disappearance is. Think about the question as you continue to read.

Chapter 19 begins with one of the longest descriptions in the book of the beauty of being on the river. It goes on for almost a third of the chapter. Near the end of this section, Huck sums up what he's been saying with, "It's lovely to live on a raft."

He meets the two new characters while paddling a canoe near the shore to look for berries. One looks to be about 70, the other about 30, and both are dressed in ragged clothes. They're in a great hurry to get away from somebody, and Huck agrees to let them come back to the raft with him.

NOTE: Since these two don't know each other, each man introduces himself by describing his line of work. If you need help with some of the skills they name, use the following list:

Temperance revival: A religous meeting at which drinking alcohol is condemned

Jour printer: A printer who travels around looking for a
day's work (jour is the French word for day)
Patent medicine: Usually a concoction of any ingredients
available, accompanied by wild claims for what it will
cure
Mesmerism: Hypnotism
Phrenology: The study of personality as it is revealed by
bumps on the skull
Laying on of hands: Curing people by touching them and
praying aloud

After the introductions there's a comical scene in
which each man claims to be descended from a noble
family. So the shabby con men miraculously become a
duke and a dauphin (the son of the deceased king of
France).

Huck, of course, is too sharp really to believe any of
this, but he has no objection to pretending, "long as it
would keep peace in the family." At the end of Chapter 19, he explains why he takes this position.

Chapter 20 shows the two con men in action as they
visit a small town and steal a few dollars. You'll also
see them planning a scene from *Romeo and Juliet*, in
which the old man (the king) will play Juliet. "These
country jakes" won't even notice anything wrong, the
duke assures him.

This chapter is important for one other development. The king has come up with a plan that will
allow them to ride the river during the day. It involves
some unpleasant news for Jim, who takes it calmly
enough. He does tell Huck at the end of the chapter,
though, that he hopes they aren't going to run into
any more kings during their trip.

CHAPTER 21

In Chapters 21 to 23 Huck tells us about his visit to a small town in Arkansas with the duke and the king. You should read these three chapters as a unit.

Chapter 21 begins with the two con men getting ready for the Shakespearean performance they intend to give in the towns they visit along the river. One of the duke's occupations, remember, was acting, so he's the resident expert on topics like the plays of Shakespeare. Of course, he doesn't know nearly as much about Shakespeare as he pretends, but he knows enough to fool the others on the raft.

Huck describes the duke's ham acting as he tries to reconstruct Hamlet's "To be or not to be" soliloquy. Finally, he says he has it, and Huck gives us the speech that he recites.

As you might expect, the soliloquy isn't quite accurate. It includes lines from *Macbeth, Romeo and Juliet,* and a few other plays, along with lines from other scenes in *Hamlet.*

Aside from what it says about the duke, the speech is a pretty good piece of comedy in its own right. If you read it aloud, and pretend that it has meaning, you might find that it actually does sound like a real speech from Shakespeare. Give Mark Twain credit for composing a good parody.

As fake as it is, Huck is impressed. Describing the duke's rendition of the speech, he says it "just knocked the spots out of any acting ever *I* see before."

In the circular that the duke prints to advertise their show, he bills himself as David Garrick and the king as Edmund Kean. Those were real people, probably the most famous Shakespearean actors of the 19th century. (The circular, by the way, has Shakespeare's name misspelled.)

Huck gives us a careful description of the town and its residents, and it sounds like an awful place. The streets are muddy, the houses are falling apart, and the stores are neglected. The men he describes are lethargic do-nothings whose main concern is where their next chew of tobacco is coming from.

In other words, Huck now finds himself in surroundings that are the direct opposite of the ones he just left—the studied gentility of the Grangerford home. You remember what Twain's comment was on that branch of society. You might think he was setting up this contrast to show how these people are different from the aristocrats he condemned earlier. But don't be too quick to jump to conclusions. Read the rest of the chapter, and the one that follows, and see how Twain has these people behave.

Huck, along with many townspeople, witnesses the cold-blooded shooting of a tough-talking drunk who insults a well-dressed man named Colonel Sherburn. Sherburn shows a little patience by giving the drunk a warning. When the warning is ignored, the colonel kills him.

The reaction of the townspeople is what this incident really is about. Notice what they do immediately after the man is shot. Watch them argue over who will get the "front-row seats" to see him take his last breath. Notice the pleasure they take in watching a reenactment of the shooting.

Then, although no one raised a finger when the shooting was taking place, they decide to mob together and lynch Colonel Sherburn. Huck doesn't comment on any of this, but you should be able to deduce how Twain feels about these people. If not, you'll find out in the next chapter.

CHAPTER 22

NOTE: If you haven't read much of Mark Twain's work, there's a good chance you have a misconception about him. To many people, he's a kind of lovable-old-uncle character who wrote great stories about a time when America was a lovely place to live in.

This image of Twain often comes from having seen movies about Tom Sawyer and Huck Finn, movies made for a family audience and therefore heavy on virtue and traditional values. Movies like these aren't necessarily distortions of what Twain wrote; but they do show only part of the truth.

The aspect of Twain that most people know nothing about is the sharp, often bitter critic of human nature. At his best, he packages the strongest criticism in humor, and makes us laugh even though we are the butt of the joke. But the humor would sometimes elude him, especially as he got older and as his life became more and more tragic. The result is often ugly, bitter comments about the human race that make you squirm as you read them.

And that's what you have at the beginning of Chapter 22. The mob goes to Sherburn's house, all full of noise and bravery. But the second he steps outside to face them, they inch back a bit. Then he makes a speech intended to shame not only the mob, but all of us, if Twain has his way.

This speech will show you what Twain could be like when he wasn't trying to be charming or funny. It may also give you a clue to why his wife disliked *The Adventures of Huckleberry Finn* so much that she tried to talk him out of publishing it.

There's one other thing the speech may do. If this side of Twain sounds interesting to you, the speech may whet your appetite for more of his thoughts on the subject. You'll find a lot of material in such works as *The Mysterious Stranger*, *The Diaries of Adam and Eve*, and *The Man That Corrupted Hadleyburg*.

When the mob disbands, Huck sneaks into a circus that's in town. We've been saying a lot about how smart Huck is, and how much wiser he is than most of the people he knows. This circus scene is a good reminder that he is also a kid with a good share of naïveté.

For someone who can see right through the two con men who have moved in with him, Huck is pretty easily fooled by the prearranged act he watches at the circus. Even when he finds out it was prearranged, he still believes that the ringmaster was fooled. In spite of everything he knows, Huck is still a simple kid.

CHAPTER 23

Although there's an abrupt shift at the end, this chapter is mostly comedy. In the first part Huck tells us of how the king and the duke con the men of the town out of nearly $500 and get away unhurt. The way they make their living prompts Jim to ask Huck if he isn't surprised at "de way dem kings carries on."

And that leads Huck into a long monologue on the terrible behavior of kings. He cites Henry VIII as a typical kingly rapscallion, then attributes to him everything he can think of from English history. This monologue is similar to the Shakespeare jumble we got earlier from the duke.

As for Twain, he's making us laugh again, even though he's commenting on yet another sad example of human folly.

The next morning Huck awakes to find Jim pining for his family. He says Jim cares for his family as much as white people care for theirs. "It don't seem natural," he adds, "but I reckon it's so."

That statement is just a reminder that Huck still doesn't think of Jim as quite human, even if he is committed to a friendship with him. But Twain isn't going to let his reader fall into the same trap.

He ends the chapter with Jim telling a harrowing story about a time he slapped his four-year-old daughter for not obeying him. The girl had just come through an attack of scarlet fever, and Jim didn't know what effect it had had on her.

When he found out—after he'd slapped her—he was overcome with grief over what he had done. He begged God to forgive him, he says, because he would never forgive himself.

Read Jim's account of this incident carefully. Try to hear him telling Huck about it. If his story doesn't remind you of how human he is, nothing ever will.

CHAPTER 24

This chapter is the beginning of the longest episode in the book, which extends from Chapter 24 to 30.

As the duke and the king lay plans to bilk some townspeople out of their money, Jim mentions that he's finding it difficult to stay tied up in the cramped quarters of the wigwam while the others are away all day. The duke comes up with a solution that allows him to show himself on the raft during daylight.

As you'll see when you read these chapters, this solution is really a plot device that solves a problem Twain had to face if he wanted to use the next episode. The swindle will keep Huck and the men in town for several days, and Twain couldn't just leave

Jim tied up in the wigwam all that time.

Huck now has some store-bought clothes the thieves were able to get with the money they took in from their Shakespearean performance. He's going to be billed as a servant. The plan is for them to hail a steamboat between towns, then arrive in the next town and claim they've traveled from St. Louis or Cincinnati.

On the way, they offer a ride to a young man who is waiting for the boat himself, and the king initiates a conversation that turns out to be very profitable for him. He learns about a villager who has just died while expecting his brothers from England. He learns that the man was wealthy, and that no one in town has ever seen the two brothers.

From there the king "casually" conducts the conversation so that he gets one useful detail after another, until the young man has told him everything. They drop the man off at the steamboat and head back upstream.

Later in the day, three people arrive in town on a steamboat from Cincinnati. The older man claims to be the Reverend Harvey Wilks. He introduces the younger man as his deaf-mute brother, William. He doesn't have to tell anyone that the young boy with them is their servant.

Huck, of course, has known all along that this is what the duke had in mind as he pumped the young man for information. Now he watches as the two imposters pretend unbearable grief at having arrived too late to console their dying brother. He sees, too, how the simple people of the town erupt with sympathy for these two saddened travelers.

"It was enough," he tells us, "to make a body ashamed of the human race."

CHAPTER 25

If the king and the duke made Huck ashamed of the human race just by fooling the townspeople, they're about to outdo themselves with the family of the dead Peter Wilks. Huck reacts to the three Wilks daughters more tenderly than he does to anyone else he meets in the book. And because of that reaction, this particular swindle causes him no end of moral grief.

If he's disgusted, then why is he going along with the masquerade? Remember, he has a friend on the raft, a friend who can't leave now that they are back in a Southern slave state. He knows what the two men—especially the king—are capable of, and he won't risk having Jim turned in to the authorities.

So for the time being at least, he has to take part in the swindle. He says several times in this chapter that he finds the thieves' behavior "disgusting" and "sickening," but he's their captive and he has to go along with them.

The "brothers" have been left $6000 in gold, which they get to examine in private. The duke wants to take off immediately, but the king is overcome by greed for all the property he can add to the gold.

He hatches a plan for winning the confidence of the three girls—and the townspeople—in the hopes of robbing the girls of everything they have. Huck relates in disgust how successful the plan is.

There is one little hitch in the plan, but the king is able to overcome it. The town doctor, who was away earlier in the day, returns as the townspeople's sympathy for the thieves is at its highest. He listens to the king for a few minutes and laughs in his face.

The doctor knows immediately that they're dealing with a couple of frauds, because he realizes what a terrible imitation of a British accent the king is doing. As a friend of the dead man, he denounces the thieves and tells the daughters to do the same.

But the girls are too deeply caught up in the mob sentiment. Mary Jane, the oldest daughter, turns down the doctor's advice and dramatically makes a presentation to the thieves to express her confidence in them. Peter Wilks' friend has been rebuffed, and the swindlers have been accepted into the dead man's family. The chapter ends with the king throwing a sarcastic remark at the doctor.

Huck's disgust at the behavior of the king and duke is easy enough to share. But if you read closely, you might see Twain expressing disgust with more than those two.

The townspeople may mean well, but Twain paints them as something less than admirable. How could anyone, for example, believe that the king's speech pattern was that of an Englishman? Once the possibility of fraud is brought to their attention by a respected citizen of the town, how could they persist, and even cheer when Mary Jane refuses to listen to the doctor?

Although the rest of this episode focuses on the king and the duke, there are occasional references to the narrow vision of the townspeople. These references are subtle, so keep an eye open for them as you read. When the episode reaches its climax in Chapter 30, Twain will drop some of the subtlety and have Huck comment openly on certain townspeople.

What it all adds up to is an indictment, not only of "rapscallions" like the king and duke, but of all of us. It's Twain momentarily forsaking the role of trenchant humorist, and airing his grievances against the human race.

CHAPTER 26

Posing as the men's valet—"valley" as he pronounces it—Huck is given a small room next to theirs for sleeping. After dinner, which is described with some humor, Huck finds himself in the kitchen with Joanna, the youngest sister.

She begins asking him questions about living in England, and Huck confidently shifts into the lying mode he is such a master of. But he's talking to someone who's bright and who knows something about England, and he soon finds that he's in over his head. He has to keep resorting to the pretense that he's choking on a chicken bone, to give himself time to think of ways out of his self-laid traps.

Mary Jane and Susan come into the kitchen as Joanna is expressing some doubt about the whopper Huck has just told her. They take her to task for being unkind to him, and Joanna offers him a touching apology.

This treatment makes him think again about what he's allowing the king and the duke to do, and he makes an important decision on the spot. He'll steal their money from the men and give it back to the girls.

While he's looking for the money, the men come upstairs and he has to hide behind a curtain. He overhears their conversation about selling the property that belongs to the girls, and he picks up a fact that will become very important before this swindle comes to an end.

With Huck listening, they hide the money inside a mattress and leave the room. Huck takes the money to his room and waits until everyone is asleep.

CHAPTER 27

Huck sneaks downstairs in the middle of the night, intent on finding a safe hiding place for the money. When he hears someone coming, he hurriedly stashes the gold in the coffin, which is only half-open, exposing the upper half of the dead man's body. He has to leave it there, even though he's afraid it will be discovered the next day by the undertaker.

The undertaker and his style of caring for the bereaved are the subject of one of the novel's funnier passages. Huck describes in some detail how the "softest, glidingest, stealthiest man I ever see" manages to conduct the funeral services while "making no more sound than a cat."

Although the coffin lid is put on without incident, Huck isn't completely sure the money is safe. He wonders if someone, maybe even the king, might have found it during the night. His plan was to write to Mary Jane after he was safely away from town, to tell her where to find the money. Now he's afraid he might be telling her to dig up nothing but the remains of her uncle.

The day after the funeral, Huck tells us, "the girls' joy got the first jolt." Their "uncles" sold the household slaves to two traders—the sons going to one and the mother to the other. The girls never imagined that the slave family would be sold to out-of-towners, much less broken up, and Huck says "they cried and took on so it most made me down sick to see it." The only thing that keeps him from breaking down is that he knows the sale is illegal and will be nullified in a few days.

Huck takes advantage of the sale to get out of his next tight spot, when the king questions him about the missing money. Since the king was inclined to distrust the slaves anyway, Huck leads him to believe that they stole his gold. Because he's sold the slaves, the king has to write the loss off as unrecoverable.

The chapter ends with Huck expressing his pleasure that "I'd worked it all off onto the niggers, and yet hadn't done the niggers no harm by it." His practical approach to morality is still much in evidence, but he's also unwilling to hurt other people when it can be avoided.

CHAPTER 28

As he's going downstairs the next morning, Huck hears Mary Jane crying in her room. He goes in to console her and learns that she's still upset about the fate of the household slaves the king has sold.

The urge to make her feel better is so strong that he does something he can't explain to himself—he tells the truth. He assures her that the slaves will be back inside of two weeks.

He's so startled by his behavior that he interrupts the narrative to wonder over it. He's puzzled by the discovery that in a tight spot it could actually be better—*safer* even— to tell the truth than to lie. He promises himself to "lay it by in my mind, and think it over some time or other, it's so kind of strange and unregular."

And then, since he's already taken the plunge, he goes on and tells Mary Jane more of the truth. He doesn't tell her everything. For example, he holds back the grisly tale of where her money is hidden, preferring to give her that information in a note; and he refers only indirectly to the reason he's bound to stay with the thieves, not mentioning that he's helping a runaway slave.

But he tells her just about everything else, and gets her to promise that she'll take part in a plan he's devised to expose the thieves, to get her money back, and to get away safely himself. The most difficult part is that she isn't to share what he's told her with her sisters or anyone else.

When they have all the details worked out, and Mary Jane is ready to leave as the plan calls for, she says goodbye by promising to pray for Huck. Give a careful reading to his reaction to that.

He compares himself to Judas, the disciple who betrayed Christ and turned him over to the Roman soldiers. As harsh as that comparison is, it's in keeping with what we've seen over and over again of Huck's self-image. He thinks praying for him is a monumental task for a mere girl to take on, "but I bet she done it, just the same—she was just that kind."

After he says that, Huck tell us how he felt then—and still feels long afterward—about Mary Jane. More than anything else, it sounds as though Huck is telling us about the first (possibly the only) person he ever loved.

His next job is getting Mary Jane's sisters to cooperate—unwittingly—with his plan. Through some harmless lying and clever manipulating, he pulls it off pretty easily. "I judged I had done it pretty neat," he says after it's all set. "I reckoned Tom Sawyer couldn't 'a' done it no neater himself."

Unfortunately, these carefully laid plans are not going to work as smoothly as Huck expected. Just as the king and duke are selling off the last pieces of the family property, a crowd comes from the steamboat landing, loudly announcing the arrival of two other men who claim to be the brothers of the deceased Peter Wilks.

CHAPTER 29

The two newcomers are, of course, the real thing, and in a sane and rational world their arrival would immediately reverse the course of events and set everything right. A work of fiction, however, isn't ruled by rationality, but by the interests of the author who created it.

Maybe it's possible to excuse the townspeople for being taken in up until now. Maybe it can be written off to a trusting nature compounded by an eagerness to see the girls taken care of. If you want to be charitable, you could say that the townspeople have acted pretty much the way any decent people would probably act in a similar situation.

But now the real brothers have arrived, now the townspeople are speaking to a parson who really speaks like a parson, and whose British accent is genuine. They might have overlooked the king's crudity before, giving him the benefit of the doubt because they believed him to be a man of religion. But can they continue to delude themselves now, in the face of the contrast between the genuine article and a patent fraud?

Well, yes, they can. And this is where Twain's trenchant comments on his fellow creatures become difficult to take with a smile. In this chapter, the people show themselves to be so thickheaded, so stupid, so blind to the most obvious evidence, that no reader could feel much sympathy for them. Not only do they fail to see the obvious; they also turn the "investigation" of the two newcomers into a circus sideshow, cheering the conflicting claims of the two pairs of men, and egging them on to further outrageous statements.

The town lawyer, who has just come back from a

business trip, joins the doctor and a few others in backing the two new arrivals. At one point these two men question Huck about England, and he finds he can't fool them as easily as he did Joanna in an earlier scene.

The lawyer lets him off gently, telling him he isn't much of a liar. "I didn't care nothing for the compliment," Huck says, "but I was glad to be let off, anyway."

The most amazing thing to Huck in this incident is how brazenly the king sticks to his imposture, no matter what evidence is produced against him. When he's tricked into writing his name, and the lawyer shows that his handwriting isn't anything like the writing in the letters Peter Wilks received from his brother, the king doesn't falter. He has an explanation.

When the real brother claims to know what was tattooed on the dead man's chest, the king challenges him with his own claim of what the tattoo is. This claim and counterclaim lead to the complete unraveling of the escape plan Huck worked out with Mary Jane.

The conflicting claims whet the people's appetite for sensation, and they jump on the suggestion that the body be dug up in order to settle the argument. Twain has now taken the townspeople beyond mere stupidity into ghoulishness, and he'll soon add blinding greed to the list of accusations he's leveling at the human race.

Huck is dragged to the cemetery, along with the cheering mob, the two imposters, and the real brothers. Since he has no chance to escape, he seems doomed to be punished for the fraud with the king and the duke.

When the coffin is raised and opened, however, the

sight of the gold entrances everyone there, including the man who has been holding Huck by the wrist. His account of escaping from the mob is a good piece of writing, filled with tension and suspense. Read it slowly to see how good it is.

Huck gets to the raft, much to the delight of Jim, who has been waiting several days without word from any of his traveling companions. Huck begs him to save the jubilation for the morning, to cut the raft loose, and get them out of there.

As they begin to move, Huck realizes that he's once again free of the civilized society he fears so much. He's thrilled to be back on the river, and he jumps and kicks his heels a few times to express his joy.

But the joy is short-lived. He soon hears "a sound that I knowed mighty well." A flash of lightning shows him that he was right—the king and the duke escaped right behind him, and they're on their way to the raft.

CHAPTER 30

As Huck might have guessed, the king and the duke were as wily as he was when it came to making a getaway. If the sight of the gold in the coffin made Huck's captor let his guard down, it did exactly the same for the two thieves.

The king's first impulse is to accuse Huck of "tryin' to give us the slip." But Huck does some fast talking, the duke comes to his defense, and the matter is quickly forgotten.

He has a close call, though, when the two men begin talking about how the gold got into the coffin. He knows they're smart enough to put two and two together, and if they figure out the truth, he's going to be in serious trouble.

He's saved by the fact that, being inveterate thieves, they know exactly how much trust to put into each other—none. Each man suspects the other of having hidden the money in the coffin, with the intention of getting it for himself at a later time.

Their mutual distrust takes the heat off Huck, and the subject doesn't come up again. When the two men drink themselves to sleep, Huck tells Jim everything that has happened.

CHAPTER 31

On this leg of their trip, things get lazy, which is fine with Huck; but they also get unprofitable, which is troublesome for the two con men. After they move far enough south to be free of any word-of-mouth that might follow them, the thieves try their hand at such things as temperance lectures, dance instruction, missionarying, mesmerizing, and doctoring.

When none of their schemes works, the two men become moody and begin talking confidentially between themselves. This bothers Huck and Jim, and for good reason, since they know the two men are capable of almost anything.

They decide that the men must be planning to rob a house or a store. This prediction shows just how naïve Huck still is, in spite of all he's experienced. What the con men are planning is far worse than a robbery, but Huck isn't able even to imagine it.

They soon stop at "a shabby village named Pikesville." The king goes in first, and Huck and the duke follow several hours later. When they get to town, they find the king drunk, and the duke begins arguing with him.

Huck doesn't waste a second. This is the time for

him and Jim to escape these two men. He takes off for the raft and never looks back.

Jim, however, is gone, and Huck soon learns that the king has identified him as a runaway slave and sold his interest in the $200 reward for $40.

Then he sits down and thinks where he is, how he got there, and what he should do next. Once again, as he did in Chapter 16, he evaluates his behavior according to the standards he's been taught to believe are correct, and he finds himself falling short. And once again, we know how wrong he is.

He considers writing to Miss Watson and telling her where Jim is, believing that Jim would be happier with his family and other people he knows. He decides against this because he believes that Miss Watson, and everyone else who knows Jim, would never again treat him well, now that he's tried to run away.

That leads him to thinking about how people are going to judge him for helping a slave to escape. He's not only convinced that he's done a serious wrong, he won't even let himself off for being brought up improperly, since he had the advantage of Sunday School and threw that advantage away.

Then he tries to pray, "but the words wouldn't come," and he thinks he knows why. "It was because my heart warn't right; it was because I warn't square; it was because I was playing double." He's trying to get God to forgive him, when he doesn't really feel sorry for helping Jim. And he realizes that "you can't pray a lie."

So he decides to do the right thing first, and pray later. He writes a note to Miss Watson, telling her where to find her runaway slave. Although this makes him feel "washed clean of sin" for the first time in his life, he puts the paper down and thinks some more. He's hoping to find some personal justification for what he's about to do.

He thinks about the trip and all the things that have happened between him and Jim, and he can't "seem to strike no places to harden me against him, but only the other kind." Jim, he decides, is a good person, who really cares for him; and the feeling is mutual.

So he takes a deep breath and says to himself, "All right, then, I'll *go* to hell." And he tears up the note to Miss Watson.

It's easy to miss the full force of the decision Huck makes in this scene. You might find it comical that he thinks helping a slave will send him to hell, and if you do, you might not realize exactly what he's saying.

Remember, he believes what he's been told in Sunday School. He believes that God will punish evil people by sending them to hell for eternity. And he believes that slavery, like other American institutions, has the Heavenly Stamp of Approval.

So he isn't using a figure of speech when he makes his decision. And he isn't being sarcastic. He's dead serious when he says he'll go to hell for not turning Jim in. Yet he decides to do it because he feels for Jim as a human being, even if all the "good" people don't—even if God Himself doesn't.

Wickedness "was in my line, being brung up to it," he says, and goodness isn't. If helping the only real friend he has is called wicked by the "civilized" people, then he'll be wicked and give up all hope of reforming.

His first really evil act, then, will be to help Jim complete his escape. To do that, he hatches a plan to get rid of the king and duke for good, and then to go to the home of Silas Phelps, the man who bought Jim from the king.

He meets the duke in town, and they exchange lies about what happened to the raft and to Jim. Since he knows more of the truth than the duke does, Huck wins this battle of wits and ends up temporarily out of danger from the two con men. That leaves him free to see what he can pull off at the Phelps home.

CHAPTER 32

Twain sets a dismal tone for this chapter with the opening paragraph, and the tone isn't made any more cheerful by the description of the Phelps home that follows. Huck enters the property without any clear plan of what he's going to do, "but just trusting to Providence to put the right words in my mouth when the time come."

In other words, God, who will send him to hell for helping Jim, will also give him the words to get the deed done. At the very least, you can say that Huck has some confused notions about how God operates.

When Huck meets the woman of the house, she thinks he's a relative that her husband has gone to meet at the steamboat. When she asks why the boat was so late, he says that a cylinder head exploded.

"Good gracious!" she says. "Anybody hurt?"

"No'm," he answers. "Killed a nigger."

It might seem like an insignificant exchange, but think about it a minute. His response to her question is exactly what a boy in his circumstances might say. It suggests a definition of black people that has nothing to do with humanity.

How does this fit with what we know of Huck? How could such a statement come from a boy who's decided to go to hell rather than betray his black friend?

The answer is important, because it will help you understand just what Huck is doing. Nothing he has said so far indicates that he's opposed to slavery, or that he wants to see an improvement in the status of black people in society. Nothing he has said even hints at any such revolutionary ideas.

Remember that Huck is just a young teenager, not a revolutionary. He isn't challenging society. He's simply choosing to live outside of it. The raft gave him a chance to do that temporarily. His decision to help Jim is a way of becoming a permanent outsider.

The woman tells him to address her as Aunt Sally, and she calls him Tom. He has trouble answering her questions, because he doesn't know where he's supposed to be from.

He finds out when her husband, Silas, comes back from the dock. Aunt Sally introduces Huck as Tom Sawyer. After that, there's no stopping Huck. He sails into stories about Tom's family and neighbors that please the dickens out of the Phelpses.

The one problem Huck sees is that if Tom Sawyer was expected, then Tom Sawyer will soon arrive. What will Aunt Sally and Uncle Silas think then? His next task is to get to the overdue steamboat when it arrives, and let Tom in on what's happening.

CHAPTER 33

Huck starts off for town and meets Tom Sawyer's wagon on the way. Tom, of course, is frightened by what he thinks is Huck's ghost, but Huck soon convinces him that he's alive and well.

When Huck explains his situation, Tom is happy to play along. Then Huck tells him that he's there to help Miss Watson's Jim escape. Tom starts to say something, then stops. After thinking for a moment, he says he'll help Huck steal Jim from his Uncle Silas.

Huck is absolutely shocked. At that moment, he says, Tom Sawyer "fell considerable in my estimation." How could Tom Sawyer, a good boy from a respectable family, agree to help Huck in his "dirty, low-down business"?

Huck isn't going to learn the answer until the end of the book, but Tom knows that Jim is already a free man. His agreeing to help Huck is a charade. He'll go through the motions of breaking the law, but he secretly knows there's nothing criminal about what they're doing. Keep this in mind as you read about the escapades Tom invents for Jim and Huck in the next several chapters.

Now that Tom has agreed to help, he and Huck work out the first part of the plan—Tom's arrival at his uncle's house. As Huck expects, Tom arrives with style, attracting the whole family outside to see who the stranger is.

After masquerading as a traveler from Ohio, he plays a trick on Aunt Sally and then announces that he is, in fact, Tom's brother Sid. This makes him even more welcome than he was before, and it also ensures that both boys will be able to stay for as long as they need to.

Huck hears that the townspeople are wise to the king and the duke, and he and Tom sneak into town at night to warn them. They get there just in time to see the men, tarred and feathered and tied to a rail, about to be run out of town.

After all the heartache the two thieves have caused Huck, the only thing he can feel for them now is sympathy. "Human beings," he tells us, "*can* be awful cruel to one another."

His sensitive conscience then begins to bother him, as though he were somehow responsible for what's happened to the two men. In the last paragraph of the chapter, he makes some comments about conscience that you might find interesting.

CHAPTER 34

Now everything is in place for the two boys to help Jim escape. In this chapter and the ones that follow, you'll see some interesting contrasts between Huck's view of the world and Tom's. You may remember some of these contrasts from the early part of the book, in which Tom spun elaborate tales about adventures, and Huck found it hard to take any of them seriously.

This chapter begins with Tom suggesting that he and Huck each think of a plan, and that they then decide which is better. Huck knows he's outclassed here, and he hardly gives any thought to a plan, convinced that Tom's will be far superior to anything he can think of.

When you read the two plans, you might not agree with Huck. The one he comes up with is practical, straightforward, and based solidly on the experiences he's recently had on the river. Even Tom agrees that it would work, but that isn't the point.

The point, according to Tom, is to have an adventure, to pull off something that has style. When he tells Huck his plan, Huck agrees that "it was worth fifteen of mine for style, and would make Jim just as free a man as mine would, and maybe get us all killed besides."

After agreeing to the plan, Huck again has qualms about involving Tom in this criminal—and sinful— business of helping Jim escape. But when he brings the subject up, Tom assures him that he knows what he's doing. Huck still doesn't understand, but he sees no way of talking Tom out of it.

The boys examine the place where Jim is being held prisoner, and Huck sees a simple way of getting him out. Tom refuses to do anything simply, and decides on an alternative that will take about a week to accomplish. By the end of the chapter, they have let Jim know that they're on the scene and that they're planning to get him out.

CHAPTER 35

The "dark, deep-laid plans" of this chapter underline the contrast between the way the two boys approach problems. Tom begins by bemoaning the fact that freeing Jim would be so simple that it would embarrass any self-respecting adventurer. Uncle Silas is so trusting, and the prison is so flimsy, that they'll have to invent difficulties that the enemy has failed to supply them.

Huck has a conflict here. On the one hand, he's in awe of Tom's ability to do things up right, to bring his personal style to everything he does. On the other hand, he wants desperately to get Jim out and run off with him.

He listens as Tom lists the complications that they'll have to create in order to make the escape worthwhile. But in spite of his esteem for Tom's style, he keeps questioning why they can't just get him out and take off.

"Why, hain't you ever read any books at all?" Tom asks in exasperation. Doesn't Huck know anything about what the "best authorities" say on the subject of escaping prisoners? Has Huck no respect for such things as rope ladders, and moats, and digging out of a prison with a fork?

The answer to all those questions is "no," of course. Huck doesn't know much at all about the play-acting kind of adventure that Tom has mastered so well. It's unfortunate—for both himself and Jim—that he sees this as a mark of his own inferiority. In spite of all the questions Huck asks, he goes along with Tom in unnecessarily complicating the escape.

Another way of looking at the contrast between them is suggested by Tom's reaction when Huck tells him that one part of his plan is foolish. "It don't make no difference how foolish it is," Tom says. "It's the right way—and it's the regular way."

This is the boy, remember, who convinced Huck to try his hand at being "sivilized." For all his bravado, for all his talk about danger and adventure, Tom is a rule follower, the opposite of a rebel. For all his wild imagination, Tom is a kid who does what he thinks should be done, not what he might like to do.

Huck has shown, even in the most serious of situations, that what should be done is of little concern to him. That's why the two of them have this continual battle over how best to carry out their plan.

By the end of the chapter Huck has been bullied once again by Tom. "It ain't no use to try to learn you nothing, Huck," he says. Then he sends him off to steal some knives that they need only to complicate what they're going to do.

And Huck does as he's told, even though one part of him knows it's just plain foolishness.

CHAPTERS 36 AND 37

For the most part, these two chapters tell in humorous detail how Tom and Huck go about putting their plan into effect. Most of the comedy comes from the fact that a large portion of what they're doing is completely unnecessary; but there's also some funny material about all the household things they steal to imitate what Tom has read in his books.

There also are passages in the chapters that reveal more about the boys' character. For example, in the early part of Chapter 36 there's a conversation in which Twain has some fun with people who live by the letter of the law, even when their own experience makes that law seem ludicrous. (Twain had strong feelings about religious fanatics, and he certainly would have included them in this group.)

After Tom and Huck dig for a long time with their small knives, Tom admits that they'll never complete the job this way. No matter what his books tell him, he knows they'll have to use more practical tools, such as shovels and picks. He admits that "it ain't right, and it ain't moral," but he sees it has to be done.

"Now you're talking!" Huck says, praising Tom for getting more level-headed all the time. The morality of it doesn't mean a thing to Huck. When he sets out to steal something, he says, all that matters to him is that he get what he's after.

Tom says that's okay for Huck because he doesn't know any better. But for a purist like himself, a certain mental reservation is necessary. He has to pretend to be doing the right thing, even if he is giving in to reality.

Read this conversation carefully, and be sure you see exactly what's going on. Don't overlook the irony in Huck's comment, "He was always just that particular. Full of principle." And notice the final punch line about coming up the stairs instead of climbing the lightning rod.

This short scene shows Mark Twain the satirist at his best. His comment on hypocrisy is sharp and piercing, but his manner is as skillful as that of a surgeon performing a difficult operation. Huck's remarks about Tom are so subtle that they could easily be missed.

CHAPTERS 38 AND 39

In these two chapters, Tom leads Huck to ridiculous lengths in his attempt to turn Jim's escape into an adventure worthy of his books. He fills Jim's cabin with snakes, spiders, and rats. He makes him draw a coat of arms and scratch out a farewell message on a stone. He gives him a plant that has to be watered with tears, and has him keep a journal on a stolen shirt.

Most of this material is narrated humorously, and it can be read for laughs. At the same time, it's all very cruel to Jim, who has the status of a stage prop in Tom's mind. It's true that Tom knows the escape is only a charade; but Jim doesn't know that, and he's being led through all these complications in the belief that they're somehow necessary to his becoming free.

Throughout all this, Huck often gets exasperated with Tom, but he never puts his foot down and demands an end to the game-playing. In spite of all Tom's foolishness, Huck still sees Tom as the superior character, as smarter, more imaginative, better educated, and more moral than he is himself.

Of course, Twain is making fun of Tom and, by extension, of people who think like him. At the beginning of Chapter 38 he shows Tom in a very unflattering light, maybe suggesting that he's exasperated himself with what his character has been doing.

It's in the coat of arms scene that Tom looks worst. His description of a coat of arms is half correct and half ridiculous, but his bluster in presenting it successfully hides that fact from Huck. There's a direct parallel between this scene and the one in which the duke faked his way through Hamlet's soliloquy. The strong implication is that Tom is somehow similar to that lowlife, who helped the king betray Huck and Jim for a few dollars.

It takes the boys three weeks to get all the needless arrangements made, and Tom caps everything off with the most ludicrous touch of all. He sends an anonymous note to his aunt and uncle, telling them when the escape is to take place. Such notes are required in the books he reads, and he won't have this escape falling short of requirements.

CHAPTERS 40 AND 41

From the point of view of an adventure novelist (or a movie director), the escape itself is "splendid," as the title of Chapter 40 suggests. From the point of view of the escapee, however, it could have been simpler, and certainly quieter.

Tom's anonymous note results in a gathering of neighboring farmers, all of them armed and anxious to face the thieves who they think are coming to steal Silas Phelps' property. Huck is frightened at the prospect of armed men trying to interfere with the escape. Tom is thrilled and wishes there were a lot more.

When they finally do pull the escape off, two factors work very much in their favor. First, it's so dark that the farmers are firing shots randomly. And second, the dogs entrusted with tracking the thieves are family dogs, and they just run right past the boys, looking for someone more exciting.

They evade the pursuers, reach the canoe Huck has hidden, and get to the island where he left the raft. It's only then that they realize that Tom has taken a bullet in the calf, a fact that pleases him mightily.

As he bandages his wound, Tom gives orders for carrying out the rest of the escape plan. Huck and Jim ignore him and consult privately about what to do.

Then Jim announces that nothing—including his own freedom—is more important than getting medical treatment for Tom's wound. This would be a noble sentiment under any circumstances, but it's even more so when you consider how badly Tom has treated Jim for the past three weeks. Huck sees Jim's position for what it is. "He was white inside," he says.

Remember, Huck's definition of blacks as property hasn't changed. He has barely given any thought to that larger social issue. What has changed in the course of the book is his attitude toward an individual black man, who has evolved in Huck's mind from a piece of property into an admirable human being.

Huck gets a doctor, but the man won't share the tiny canoe with him. So Huck ends up back at Aunt Sally's while the doctor goes to the island to treat Tom.

Most of the rest of the chapter consists of comical comments by women of the neighborhood on the odd things that were found in the cabin after Jim escaped. They're convinced that it was the work of a crazy person, and that it must have taken a houseful of slaves four weeks to get it all done.

CHAPTERS 42 AND 43

Before Huck can get back to the raft, Tom and Jim are brought home by the doctor and a crowd. Jim's hands are tied, and Tom is carried on a mattress. In explaining how he managed to recapture the runaway slave, the doctor asks that Jim be treated well, since he showed more interest in Tom's health than he did in his own escape.

The farmers take the doctor's advice, and Huck tells us, "every one of them promised, right out and hearty, that they wouldn't cuss him no more." He notes that they weren't moved enough to remove Jim's chains or give him some decent food, but he figures he should leave well enough alone.

What follows is a wrapup of the plot, moving at breakneck speed and leaving no loose ends. Tom tells Aunt Sally how he and Huck engineered the escape. Tom's Aunt Polly arrives to tell Aunt Sally who her two guests really are. Tom announces that Jim has been a free man for two months. And Jim reveals that Huck's father is dead. This last bit of news means that Huck's $6000 is still waiting for him at home.

"Home," that is, as far as everyone is concerned, except Huck. As much as they seem to care for him, Huck isn't at all sure he belongs with these people— or any other people, for that matter. He's had some good glimpses of civilization on his journey up and down the river, and most of what he's seen hasn't been very pretty.

So the last thing he tells us is that he intends to "light out for the territory," that part of the country that hasn't yet been blessed with statehood, or with civilization.

Huck has had it with civilization. "I been there before," he says, and it doesn't have much to offer him.

A STEP BEYOND

Tests and Answers
TESTS

Test 1

1. Huck was living with the Widow Douglas _____
   because
   A. she was taking care of his money
   B. she wanted to civilize him
   C. he wanted to belong to a family
   D. he was jealous of Tom Sawyer

2. The hair-ball oracle incident shows us that _____
   A. Huck is not superstitious
   B. Jim is not superstitious
   C. both of them are superstitious
   D. Jim is superstitious, but Huck isn't

3. When Pap first comes back, he is _____
   A. angry about Huck's new life
   B. proud of Huck's recent change
   C. sad about what he's done to Huck
   D. hoping to turn over a new leaf

4. Huck escapes from his father by _____
   A. wearing a disguise
   B. getting help from Judge Thatcher
   C. burning down his father's house
   D. pretending he has been murdered

5. When Jim admits running away, Huck's first _____
   reaction is
   A. shock
   B. amusement
   C. puzzlement
   D. disinterest

6. Which of these tests did Huck *not* fail when he _____
   tried to pass himself off as a girl?
   A. threading a needle
   B. walking in high heels
   C. throwing a heavy object
   D. catching something in his lap

7. Jim's feeling about King Solomon is that he _____
   A. had a sense of humor
   B. was a wise man
   C. was anything but wise
   D. was a good ruler

8. After Jim and Huck are separated in a fog _____
   A. Huck decides never to leave Jim again
   B. Jim makes fun of Huck for being afraid
   C. they leave the raft for good
   D. Huck tells Jim it was all a dream

9. Huck thinks the Grangerfords are _____
   A. a fine, cultured family
   B. a family with no taste
   C. dishonest in business
   D. enemies of religion

10. Stephen Dowling Bots died by _____
    A. being caught in a burning building
    B. getting pneumonia
    C. standing up to a man with a gun
    D. falling down a well

11. In what ways is Huck a perceptive and observant narrator? In what ways is he naïve and unreliable?

12. What are Huck's contrasting attitudes toward lying?

13. Show how Huck's language changes when he gives detailed descriptions of the river.

14. How does Huck deal with people who disagree with

him? How did he develop such an attitude, and what does it show about how he approaches the world?

15. Is Jim a three-dimensional character, or is he a stereotypical slave?

Test 2

1. After shooting Boggs, Colonel Sherburn   _____
   A. stands up to the lynch mob
   B. leaves town
   C. forms a posse to fight the mob
   D. apologizes to the dead man's daughter

2. In talking to Jim about kings, Huck says that   _____
   kings
   A. aren't very interesting
   B. are admirable men
   C. cause trouble everywhere they go
   D. are usually unhappy

3. The king and the duke learn about the Wilks   _____
   family from
   A. the local newspapers
   B. a riverboat captain
   C. a friendly preacher
   D. a young man who's leaving town

4. Huck hides a stolen bag of gold in a   _____
   A. graveyard
   B. coffin
   C. cellar
   D. barn

5. Of all the people in the Wilks family, Huck is   _____
   most attracted to
   A. Joanna
   B. Peter
   C. Susan
   D. Mary Jane

6. The king sells Jim to   _____
   A. Silas Phelps
   B. Doctor Robinson
   C. Harvey Wilks
   D. Levi Bell

7. When Huck sees what finally happens to the   _____
   king and the duke, he
   A. feels sorry for them
   B. laughs at them
   C. speaks up against them
   D. defends them publicly

8. Tom agrees to help Jim because   _____
   A. he knows Jim is really free anyway
   B. he has learned to hate slavery
   C. he enjoys breaking the law
   D. he wants Huck to get arrested

9. When Tom thinks about how easy it will be to   _____
   rescue Jim, he
   A. tells Huck to stop worrying
   B. invents difficulties
   C. gets suspicious
   D. loses interest in the plan

10. After his escape, Jim is recaptured because   _____
    A. he loses his way in the woods
    B. he comes back to rescue Huck
    C. he refuses to leave while Tom is sick
    D. the sherrif recognizes him as a runaway

11. What changes are there in Huck's feelings about the king and the duke, from their first arrival on board to the end of the novel?

12. Show how Huck's feelings about the Grangerfords change from the time he meets them until the time he leaves.

13. Trace Huck's feelings about slavery throughout the book, and show how they do or do not parallel his feelings about Jim.

14. Explain why you think the whole book is either optimistic or pessimistic about human nature.

15. Write a character sketch of Huck as a young man.

ANSWERS

Test 1

1. B   **2.** C   **3.** A   **4.** D   **5.** A   **6.** B
7. C   **8.** D   **9.** A   **10.** D

11. Before you look back into the book for information on a question like this one, trust your memory to get you started. Make a list of some of the sharp-eyed observations you remember Huck making (many will be humorous), and a separate list of cases where he missed what was really going on.

    The first list might include his comparing Tom Sawyer's fantasizing with Sunday School and his observation that "you can't pray a lie." The second list could start with his evaluation of the Grangerfords' household and his general attitude toward Tom Sawyer.

    After you start the lists on your own, look through the chapter headings to refresh your memory about things Huck comments on. You'll probably find more examples than you'll need for an essay. When you've collected five or six examples for each list, you can begin a first draft of a paragraph (or more) for each one. For each example you should mention the observation Huck makes, explain the setting, if it's important, and show how Huck's comment is either a sharp observation or a naïve one.

12. One way to approach this question is to list all the incidents you can remember that involved Huck lying or talking about lying. The earliest mention of lying is when Huck turns his money over to the judge so he won't have to tell a lie to his father. He's also reluctant to lie to the two men on the river who ask if Jim is a runaway slave.

   On the other hand, he lies to many of the people he meets, and usually with the style of a veteran. You'll find plenty of examples of incidents when a respect for the truth seemed the farthest thing from his mind.

   To answer the question, you'll have to find the distinction between the lies he tells readily and those that trouble him. It would help if your reread "You Can't Pray a Lie." In that chapter Huck talks at length about truth, and you'll find some clues to his real feelings about lying.

13. For a good example of what happens to Huck's language when he talks of the river, reread the beginning of Chapter 12, up to the sentence, "Take it all around, we lived pretty high." Then read a section in which he describes events, like the scene in Chapter 19 when the duke and dauphin first come to the raft.

   In the river scene, you'll find many references to concrete details, like the size of the river, the sounds Huck hears, the lights of a town, the names of foods. All these sense details make you see and hear, and often taste and smell, the things Huck experiences.

   In contrast, the "action" scenes are dominated by dialogue and events. The language is plain, direct, and matter-of-fact, with little or no physical detail.

14. At one point, when he's especially annoyed by the con men, Huck says he learned from living with his father that it's best not to argue with people who take firm stands on things. That answers the first two parts of the

question. The third part will take some thought.

If he'd rather not deal with people who stand on principle, or honor, or anything else, then he probably isn't very deeply committed to anything himself. He'd never try to argue anyone out of a belief, and he expects others to leave him alone in return. In other words, his tolerance doesn't come from being broad-minded; it comes from not caring about much beyond his immediate needs and desires.

15. Early in the book, Jim has all the earmarks of a stereotype. He seems to be a caricature instead of a real person. He's overly humble, he obeys the boys in spite of his age, he's foolishly superstitous, and for a grown man, he's very dependent on Huck.

It probably would have been easy to find such characteristics in many 19th-century slaves; but if Twain's portrait went no deeper than this, it would be a stereotype, even if it was based on truth. The portrait of Jim, though, goes much deeper.

Jim's determination to earn enough money to buy his wife and children makes a sharp contrast with the shuffling slave we might have thought he was. His anger at Huck for playing a cruel joke shows his excessive humility to be just a veneer he's been taught to wear. And the feeling he expresses for Huck and for his family are so moving that they lead Huck eventually to risk going to hell to help him.

Test 2
1. A   2. C   3. D   4. B   5. D   6. A
7. A   8. A   9. B   10. C

11. To answer a question like this, you should quickly look through all the chapters involving the king and duke.

This will remind you of what happens with the two of them, and it will occasionally bring to mind a comment Huck makes on the men.

At first, Huck is more or less accepting of them, because he's accepting of most of what comes his way. He gets some amusement out of watching them work their skills, even though he feels sorry for the people they're bilking.

With the Wilks girls, he becomes disgusted with the men, even feeling ashamed at one point to be a member of the human race. But when he sees them getting what they deserve near the end of the book, he feels sorry for them.

When you write about a developing process like this one, you should include comments on what the process means. For example, you could show how each change in Huck's attitude illustrates something about his personality.

12. You should approach this question the same way you did the previous one. It's important to be specific about Huck's feelings and how they change, but the key is in drawing some conclusions about him from the changes. In the case of the Grangerfords, his attitude slowly changes from reverence to disgust, and the reasons for the change say a lot about him.

13. This essay topic might sound easier than it really is. If you were to start writing without thinking about it, you might confuse Huck's feeling for Jim with an emerging opposition to slavery. That wouldn't be doing Huck justice.

Huck never does develop an opposition to the institution of slavery. Until the end of the book, he believes that slavery is as American as democracy. The important thing about his helping Jim is that he's doing it *in spite of* his beliefs. His affection leads him to do some-

thing he considers morally wrong. The affection is so
powerful, however, that he shrugs off what might happen to him.

An answer to this question, therefore, would probably show a contrast between his feelings for Jim and his
beliefs about slavery. It would probably include a reference to an ironic scene in Chapter 32. Huck has come to
the Phelps farm to help Jim escape. But take another
look at what he says when Aunt Sally asks him if anyone was hurt in the steamboat explosion. It will show
you how far he *hasn't* come in his feelings about
slaves.

14. There is rarely a single "right answer" to an essay question, and that is most true of topics like this one. It's
possible to make a case for either side, and the strength
of the case will depend entirely on the evidence you
collect and how well you present the argument.

The more obvious evidence probably favors pessi-
mism. Twain covers almost every class of society—from
the Grangerfords to simple villagers—and he attacks
just about everyone he writes about. Huck is happy
only when he's on the raft, away from people, who
seem to cause him nothing but trouble. And Huck's
desire at the end of the book to light out for the Territory
certainly doesn't express much hope for "civilization."

But Twain doesn't attack everyone in this novel. Miss
Watson seems sincere (even if she's misguided) in her
attempts to help Huck. Judge Thatcher keeps Huck's
money aside for him, even though it has been legally
signed over to him. Uncle Silas and Aunt Sally are about
as good-hearted as two people can be. And there's
Mary Jane Wilks, a girl who causes Huck to become
almost as poetic as the Mississippi River does.

15. I can give you only a bit of help with this kind of question, and then you'll be on your own. My advice is that you base everything you say on something you find in the book. Take things that Huck says and does, and show how they will develop into adult characteristics. Or show how he must necessarily discard or alter his beliefs as he gets older.

   If you can do that, you'll have a defensible character sketch. Don't be surprised if your adult character ends up sounding suspiciously like Mark Twain.

Term Paper Ideas

1. What is Huck's attitude toward religion as it is practiced (and taught) by people like Miss Watson?

2. What is Huck's attitude toward his father? Explain how this attitude is or is not reflected in the way he deals with other people in the novel.

3. How are Huck and Tom different in the way they look at the world?

4. Trace Twain's development of Jim from the foolish character in the second chapter to the character who is sold to Silas Phelps.

5. Select one or more comic scenes from the novel and show how Twain structures them to make you laugh.

6. Show how Huck's attitude toward Jim does or does not change in the course of the book.

7. Show how Huck's attitude toward the institution of slavery does or does not change in the course of the book.

8. What is the role of superstition in the lives of the major characters in the novel?

9. How does Twain separate himself from Huck when he describes the Grangerfords' home?

10. Show how Huck's feeling for the Grangerfords changes from admiration to disgust in Chapter 19.

11. Why did Huck allow the duke and dauphin to join them on the raft, even though he knew they were crooks?

12. Explain why you think Colonel Boggs is a hero or a villain in Twain's eyes.

13. Show how Huck's grasp of history in Chapter 23 is less firm than he wants Jim to believe.

14. How does the king get the information he needs to set up the swindle of the Wilks girls?

15. How does Mark Twain show human nature in a bad light in Chapter 25? Include references to the way the king pretends to be an Englishman.

16. Trace the development of Huck's feelings for Mary Jane Wilks.

17. How does Twain portray the undertaker at Peter Wilks' funeral as a comic character?

18. What are Huck's conflicting attitudes toward telling the truth?

19. How does Huck evaluate himself morally? What basis does he have for his evaluation?

20. How does Huck evaluate himself in terms of Tom Sawyer?

21. How do you think Twain feels about Huck and about Tom?

22. Explain how Huck gets to be mistaken for Tom, and Tom for his brother Sid.

23. Show the similarity between Huck's final evaluation of the duke and king, and his feelings about his father and the thieves he runs into on the *Walter Scott*.

24. Explain why you think the long "escape-plan" episode is a good or bad way to end the novel.

25. What do you think Huck will do immediately after the end of the story?

Further Reading

CRITICAL WORKS

Baldanza, Frank. *Mark Twain: An Introduction and Interpretation*. New York: Barnes & Noble, 1961.

_____"The Structure of Huckleberry Finn." *American Literature* 27 (November 1955): 347–55.

Blair, Walter. *Mark Twain and Huck Finn*. Berkeley: University of California Press, 1960.

Brooks, Van Wyck. *The Ordeal of Mark Twain*. New York: E. P. Dutton, 1920.

Cox, James M. "Remarks on the Sad Initiation of Huckleberry Finn." *Sewanee Review* (Summer 1954): 389–405.

Fiedler, Leslie A. *Love and Death in the American Novel*, 3d ed. Briarcliff Manor, N.Y.: Stein and Day, 1982.

Marks, Barry. *Mark Twain's Huckleberry Finn*. Lexington, Mass.: D. C. Heath, 1959.

Marx, Leo. "Mr. Eliot, Mr. Trilling, and Huckleberry Finn." *American Scholar* 22 (Autumn 1953): 423–40.

Smith, Henry Nash, ed. *Mark Twain: A Collection of Critical Essays*. Englewood Cliffs, N.J.: Prentice-Hall, 1963.

AUTHOR'S OTHER WORKS (SELECTED)

The Celebrated Jumping Frog and Other Sketches (1867)

This is a collection of stories drawn from Twain's experiences while he was a reporter in the West. It includes retellings of "tall tales" and brief anecdotes centered on eccentric frontier characters.

The Innocents Abroad (1869)

This is Twain's first travel book, and the early basis of his reputation as a writer. It's a collection of humorous commentaries on his trip to Europe and Jerusalem in 1867.

Roughing It (1872)

This is an account of Twain's westward journey in the early 1860s from St. Louis, through Nevada, on to San Francisco, and to the Sandwich Islands. Like *The Innocents Abroad*, the book has Twain's sharp humor running through it.

The Gilded Age (1873)

Twain's first novel, coauthored with Charles Dudley Warner, it's about the shakeup in American values and traditions that followed the Civil War. Its title has been used by historians to label that period in American history.

The Adventures of Tom Sawyer (1876)

Twain's "hymn to boyhood," it is now thought of mostly as a children's book. It was, however, the precursor to Twain's most important work, *The Adventures of Huckleberry Finn*.

A Tramp Abroad (1880)

This is an account of a walking trip Twain took through Europe in 1879.

The Prince and the Pauper (1882)

This is an extended commentary on social classes. The plot deals with a monumental prank that backfires. When the young king of England meets a beggar who looks just like him, the king insists that they change places as a joke. The prank works so well that the boys can't get anyone to believe who they really are.

Life on the Mississippi (1883)

This is an autobiographical account of Twain's early life, during which he learned to be a riverboat pilot. The second half tells of the trip he made back home looking for material he could use in future books.

A Connecticut Yankee in King Arthur's Court (1889)

This is a satire in which a mechanic is knocked unconscious and wakes up in the court of King Arthur. He meets Merlin, Lancelot, Galahad, and other famous characters from that era, and Twain gets a chance to make fun of the romanticized Arthurian legends he found so irritating.

The Tragedy of Puddn'head Wilson (1894)

This is a relentless—and unhumorous—attack on slavery. It deals with a murder trial in Missouri in the 1830s (the time of Huck Finn's story). The identity of the killer is entwined with the question of race.

The Man That Corrupted Hadleyburg and Other Stories and Essays (1900)

The title story contains some of the bitterest comments Twain ever made on the human race. It deals with a town widely known for its honesty, and a man determined to corrupt its inhabitants because some of them had treated him badly.

The Mysterious Stranger (1916)

This is Twain's most pessimistic work. It's a series of diatribes against the weakness, stupidity, and greed that he felt characterized the human race, and notes the pointlessness of human existence.

Mark Twain's Autobiography (1924)

This is more a collection of pieces about the author than a real autobiography. Still, many people consider it a great book because of its humor, its perceptive comments on dozens of topics, and the style that made Mark Twain one of America's best writers.

The Critics

Because Huck tells his story himself, the stylistic richness is immeasurably deepened by the rhythms, intonations, and choice of words of this magnificent child.

—*Frank Baldanza*, Mark Twain, *1961*

His fresh handling of the materials and techniques of backwoods story-tellers is the clearest example in our history of the adaptation of a folk art to serious literary uses.

—*Henry Nash Smith*, Mark Twain, *1963*

Mark Twain, in short, who as a personality could not help but be a humorist, as a literary artist whose works were channeled by such currents, could not help but be an American humorist. His works are, in a sense, a summary of nineteenth-century native American humor.

—*Walter Blair*, Mark Twain and Huck Finn, *1960*

The Adventures of Huckleberry Finn is a book, rare in our literature, which manages to suggest the lovely possibilities of life in America without neglecting its terrors.

—*Leo Marx*, "Mr. Eliot, Mr. Trilling, and Huckleberry Finn," *1953*

The Adventures of Huckleberry Finn is one of those rare books which are at once acceptable to the intelligentsia and to that celebrated American phenomenon, the average citizen; it is a book which even anti-literary children read and enjoy. Even if the language of the book should eventually be lost or, worse still, replaced by convenient abridgements, the memory of Huck Finn would still survive among us like some old and indestructible god.

—*James M. Cox*, "Remarks on the Sad Initiation of Huckleberry Finn," *1955*

Clemens was sole, incomparable, the Lincoln of our literature.

> —*William Dean Howells, in* Mark Twain's Huckleberry Finn, *1959*

I think he mainly misses fire. I think his life misses fire; he might have been something; but he never arrives.

> —*Walt Whitman, in* Mark Twain's Huckleberry Finn, *1959*

All modern American literature comes from one book by Mark Twain called *Huckleberry Finn*. If you read it you must stop where the Nigger Jim is stolen from the boys. That is the real end. The rest is just cheating. But it's the best book we've had. All American writing comes from that. There was nothing before. There has been nothing as good since.

> —*Ernest Hemingway, in* Mark Twain's Huckleberry Finn, *1959*

Huck Finn is alone: there is no more solitary character in fiction. The fact that he has a father only emphasizes his loneliness; and he views his father with a terrifying detachment. So we come to see Huck himself in the end as one of the permanent symbolic figures of fiction; not unworthy to take a place with Ulysses, Faust, Don Quixote, Don Juan, Hamlet and other great discoveries that man has made about himself.

> —*T.S. Eliot, in* Mark Twain's Huckleberry Finn, *1959*

In one sense, *Huckleberry Finn* seems a circular book, ending as it began with a refused adoption and a projected flight; and certainly it has the effect of refusing the reader's imagination passage into the future. But there is a break-through in the last pages, especially in the terrible sentence which begins, "But I reckon I got to light out for the territory ahead of the rest. . . ." In these words, the end of childhood is clearly signaled; and we are forced to ask the question, which, duplicitously, the book refuses to answer: what will become of Huck if he persists in his refusal to return to the place where he has been before?

—*Leslie A. Fiedler*, Love and Death in the American Novel, *1982*